# ARCHI-
# DOODLE
# CITY

MW00487740

**LAURENCE KING**

Published in 2017
by Laurence King Publishing Ltd
361–373 City Road
London EC1V 1LR
Tel +44 20 7841 6900
Fax +44 20 7841 6910
E enquiries@laurenceking.com
www.laurenceking.com

Copyright © 2017 Steve Bowkett

Steve Bowkett has asserted his right under the Copyright, Designs and Patent Act 1988 to be identified as the Author of this work.

All rights reserved. No part of this publication may be reproduced or transmitted in any form or by any means, electronic or mechanical, including photocopy, recording or any information storage and retrieval system, without prior permission in writing from the publisher.

A catalogue record for this book is available from the British Library

ISBN 978 178067 608 1

Designed by Matt Cox for Newman and Eastwood
Cover concept by Pentagram
Project editor: Gaynor Sermon
Printed in China

# ARCHI-DOODLE CITY

## AN ARCHITECT'S ACTIVITY BOOK

STEVE BOWKETT

LAURENCE KING PUBLISHING

Known as 'the Manhattan of the desert', Shibam in the Yemen has around 500
tower blocks made from mud bricks, which rise between five and eleven storeys
high. The towers have been rebuilt many times, from the sixteenth century
onwards. Shibam is one of the first and best examples of dense urban planning.

# Introduction

More than half of the world's population now lives in urban centres across the globe, and this figure is increasing every year. Dealing with booming populations and reinventing how we live in cities is at the heart of how many architects and urban planners spend their time. *Archidoodle City* takes a look at how cities were in the past, and imagines how they may be in the future. Like my first book, *Archidoodle*, this is an activity book that invites you to design, sketch, colour and doodle different aspects of architecture, but this time the focus is on the city. I have used a broad spectrum of cities and their details as the starting point for each challenge: these range from ancient to contemporary, from small to large scale, and the challenges include both the academic and the playful, with the overriding focus being on having fun while you draw.

You are free to draw in any style and using any medium you please. All of my drawings are fairly clean and neat, but this is for the sake of clarity and you are encouraged to experiment with different tools in and around the spaces provided. As all of the drawings are black and white, feel free to use this as a colouring book instead of, or as well as, completing the exercises. Many students have found *Archidoodle* to be a useful portfolio primer, and I hope that *Archidoodle City* will be equally valuable in inspiring all readers to draw and to dream about the future of our urban environment.

**About the author**

Steve Bowkett is passionate about good design. He has taught and practised architecture for over 25 years in numerous universities and colleges and is currently a senior lecturer at London South Bank University in the UK. Steve studied architecture at the Royal College of Art in London and the Polytechnic of Central London. His previous book, *Archidoodle*, has been published in ten languages.

Steve lives in Buckinghamshire with his wife Jane and their daughters, Zoe, Sadie and Phoebe, plus a dog, two cats and a hundred fish. Steve, while still in pursuit of a serendipitous life, occasionally finds time to do nothing.

# Equipment

These are the basic tools that you might consider using in this book.

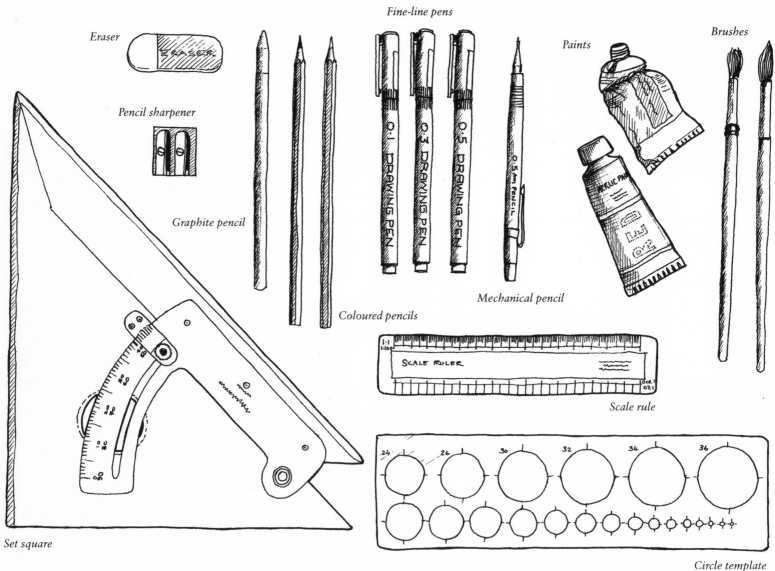

Eraser

Pencil sharpener

Graphite pencil

Fine-line pens

Coloured pencils

Mechanical pencil

Paints

Brushes

Set square

Scale rule

Circle template

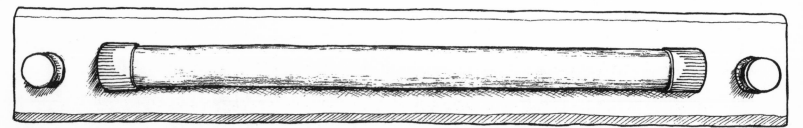

Rolling parallel rule

# Techniques

This page shows a selection of the techniques that I have used to create the drawings in this book. These simple skills will provide you with the means to build texture and form, add shadow and increase density, and create a range of different material effects.

*Hatching*

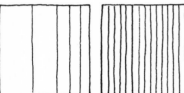 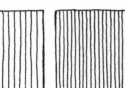 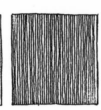 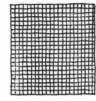

*Cross hatching*

*Stippling techniques*

     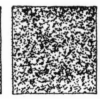  

*Material effects: coral; sediment; grasses; gravel; foliage; vegetation; rippled water; surface texture; still water*

 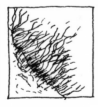      

*Material effects: water; cement render (stucco); roof tiles; planting; paving; masonry; fabric; rocks*

   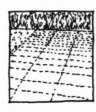 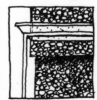  

# Sketch perspectives

These notes are a guide and not a comprehensive instruction on how to draw in perspective. The one-point perspective is often utilized to show the interior of a space – in the example below this is the interior of a street. For a one-point perspective, all elements within the drawing will converge towards a single point on the horizon (the vanishing point), which corresponds to the centre of the viewer's eye. As elements within the drawn landscape get further away they appear to get closer together and smaller.

*One-point perspective*

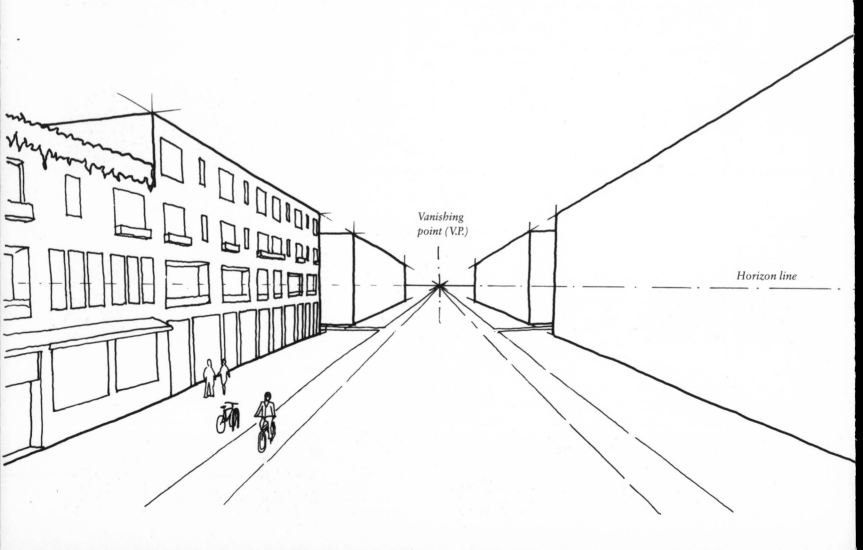

Vanishing point (V.P.)

Horizon line

The two-point perspective is useful for showing buildings as objects in three dimensions. These examples show how the horizon line (or eye line) alters the viewer's relationship to the building (i.e. looking up or down upon it) if it is moved. As you can see, there are now two vanishing points, which are both placed on the horizon line. The vertical building lines are all at right angles to the horizon line and parallel with each other. Moving the two vanishing points closer towards each other will distort the building, having the effect of making it appear to be oblique. On the other hand, moving them apart will flatten the image out.

*Two-point perspectives*

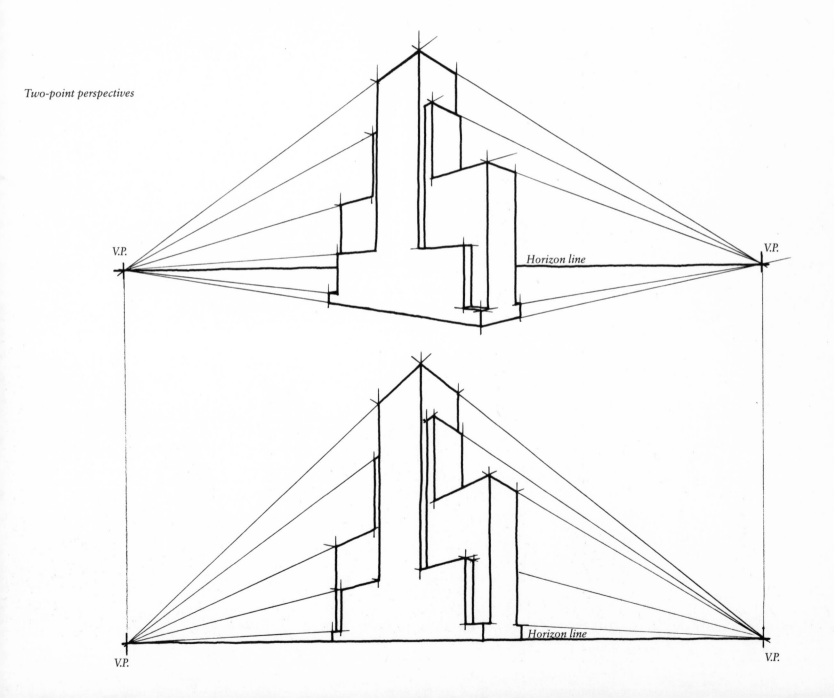

V.P.

Horizon line

V.P.

V.P.

Horizon line

V.P.

This waterfront panorama of the **city of Shanghai** in China is in a constant state of flux, with new buildings changing the skyline every year.

*In the space provided, how would you alter the character of this city?*

Shopping and **shop fronts** form a major part of our experience of cities. Here are some examples of shop fronts that either celebrate or disregard the goods or services being sold.

*In the space provided, design a shop front for a particular specialist item.*

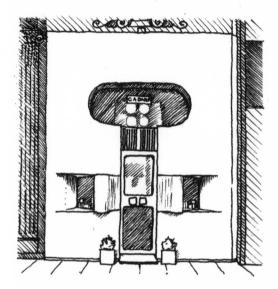

*Left: Salon Mittermeier hair salon, Linz, Austria. Xarchitekten, 2008.*
*Above: Retti candle shop, Vienna, Austria. Hans Hollein, 1965.*
*Below: Konzepp Store, clothing retailer, Hong Kong. Geoff Tsui, 2010.*

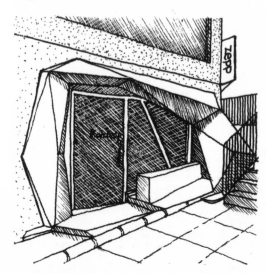

# Derinkuyu Underground City

**Derinkuyu Underground City** is an ancient (eighth to seventh century BCE) underground city of the Median Empire in the Derinkuyu district of Turkey's Nevsehir province. Extending down over many storeys to a depth of around 60 metres (200 feet), it was large enough to shelter at least 20,000 people, together with their livestock and food supplies. This is the largest excavated underground city in Turkey and is just one of several underground complexes found across the Cappadocia region.

*Complete this sectional drawing with your own underground city.*

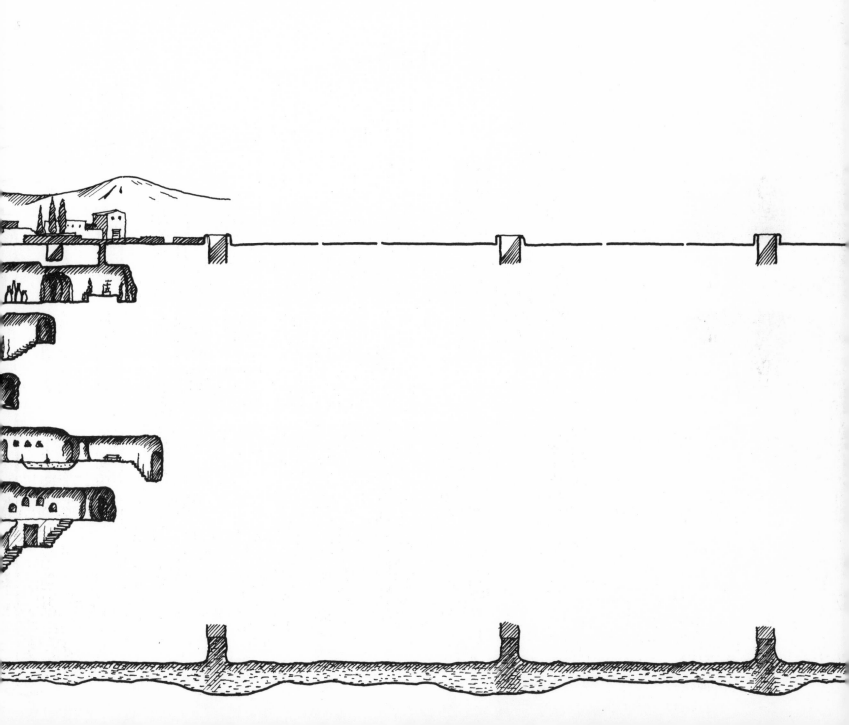

The question of **urban context** within cities has always been a much-debated issue. This example of a remodelled brownstone, designed by architect Edward Durrell Stone for his own use in 1956 in New York City, has been the subject of much controversy due to its stark contrast with its neighbours. It is currently protected as an official city landmark.

*Using the gaps in the terrace, what kind of facades will you design? Contextual? Or non-contextual?*

These silhouettes depict **famous cities.** Can you name them, and devise your own city images?

*Sketch out your own city silhouettes and try to invent some memorable iconic forms.*

The **Hoover Dam Bypass Bridge** (officially the Mike O'Callaghan–Pat Tillman Memorial Bridge) is an arch bridge that spans 323 metres (1060 feet) across the Colorado River between Arizona and Nevada. The bridge was constructed to re-route US Route 93 away from the top of the Hoover Dam, and it was completed in 2010.

*Given the opportunity to design such a significant structure, what kind of bridge would you design?*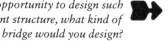

My daughter Phoebe and I decided to make a **model city** using utensils, containers and condiments from the kitchen. This partially completed drawing is one half of what we did.

*Try repeating the exercise and then add your own version to my drawing!*

Above the rooftops of Manhattan is a landscape dominated by an estimated 17,000 **water towers.**
With the majority still in use (a few have been converted into roof extensions) an educational group came up with the idea of using them as a canvas to promote the global water crisis. In 2014 'the Water Tank Project' was launched and invited over 100 acclaimed artists and New York City public school students to propose a series of wraparound artworks to cover these structures as part of this awareness campaign.

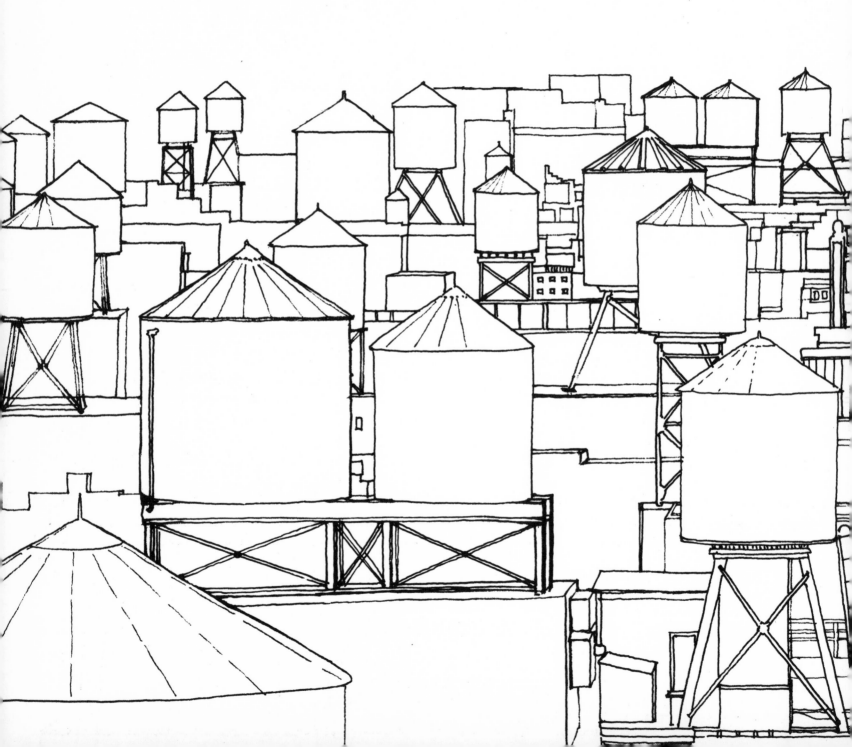

*How would you advertise this issue, or
another public issue, on this blank canvas of
water towers?*

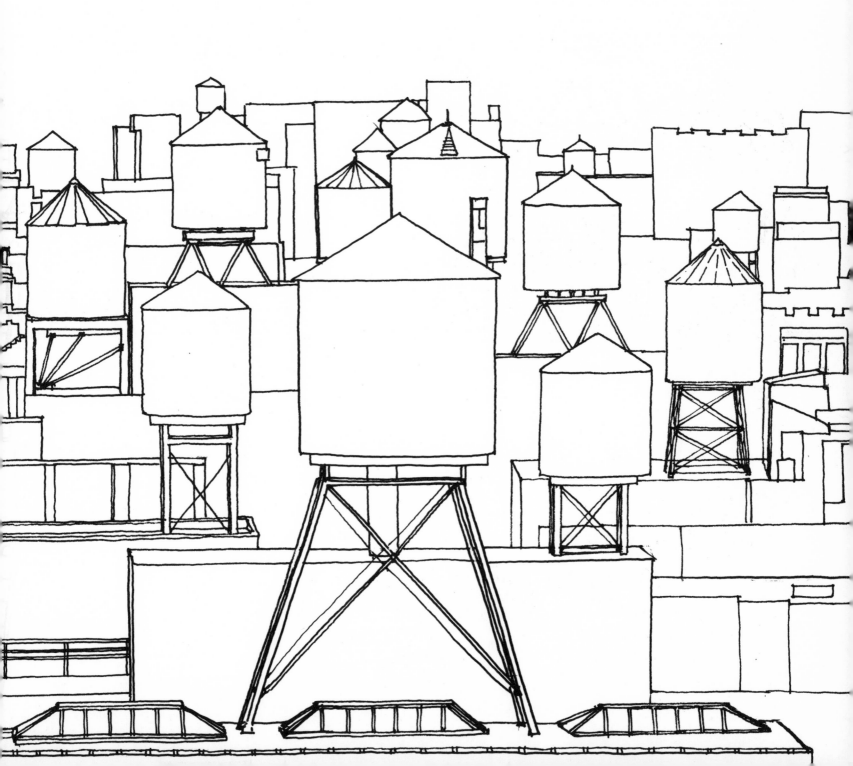

In recent years the simple **public bench** has literally taken a twist. These three examples elevate this humble and pragmatic piece of street furniture to the level of sculpture.

*'Spaghetti' bench, Pablo Reinoso, 2006.*

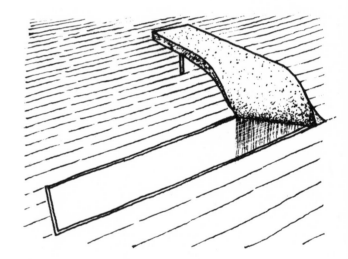

*'The Blue Carpet' bench, Heatherwick Studio, 2002.*

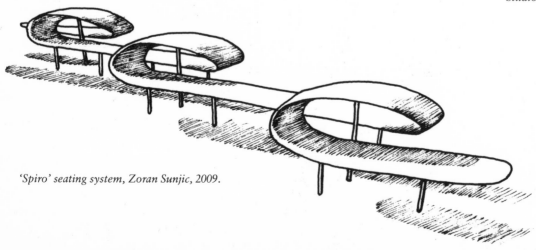

*'Spiro' seating system, Zoran Sunjic, 2009.*

*If you were commissioned to design a sculptural public bench, what would it look like? Consider materials and everyday wear and tear.*

This famous architects' costume party, **the Beaux-Arts Ball,**
held in New York in 1931, invited the designers to dress up as their own buildings.

*Design and sketch a building that you would like to be on the template provided.* ⏩

*Ely Jacques Kahn as the Squibb Building,
William Van Alen as the Chrysler Building
and Ralph Walker as No. 1 Wall Street.*

*Opposite: Ionic column
dress from David Byrne's
1986 film 'True Stories'.*

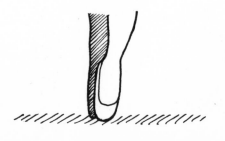

Positioned in one corner of Trafalgar Square, London, **the Fourth Plinth** remained devoid of a sculpture for 150 years after its creation. In 1999 the Royal Society of Arts decided, rather than commission a permanent sculpture, they would use the plinth to display temporary artworks by a succession of artists.

*What would you design for the Fourth Plinth?*

*'Monument'. Rachel Whiteread, 2001.*

*'Hahn/Cock'. Katharina Fritsch, 2013.*

The 180 **towers of Medieval Bologna,** built in Italy between the twelfth and thirteenth centuries, are believed to have been constructed by wealthy feuding Bolognese families. The absence of state control gave way to a lawless society in which the families needed to build taller and taller towers to defend themselves against each other. Alas, only two towers now remain. Imagine what the city would be like now if the towers had survived. Maybe new friendships would have formed?

*How would you reconnect the city's families?*
*Perhaps with different kinds of bridges*
*spanning the towers?*

# The **Nakagin Capsule Tower,** designed by Kisho Kurokawa,

was completed in Tokyo, Japan, in 1972. This building is one of the few remaining examples of
Japanese Metabolism and was the first permanent example of capsule architecture. The living
capsules measure 2.3 x 3.8 x 2.1 metres ( 7½ x 12½ x 7 feet) and are attached to two concrete
service towers.

*What living units would you connect to*
*the two vertical stair and lift towers?*

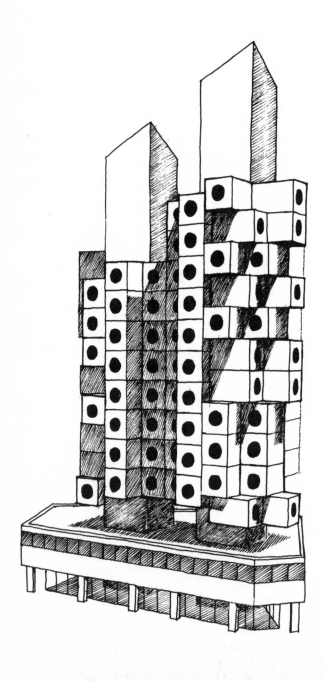

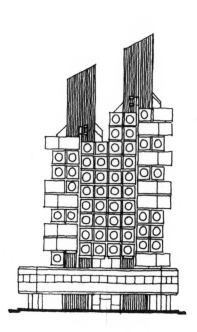

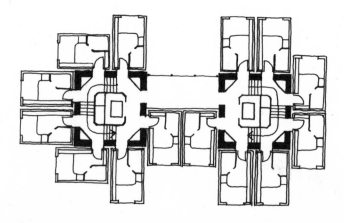

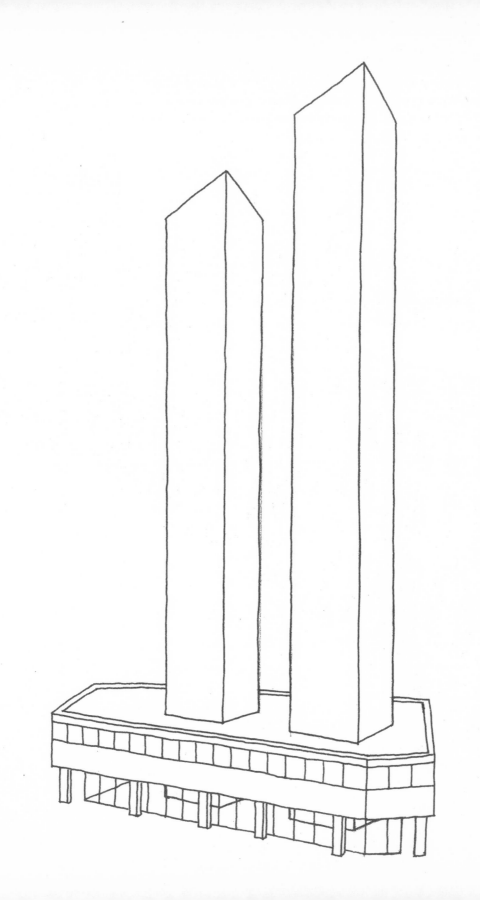

# Somerset House,

built in 1776 by Sir William Chambers, is a large neoclassical courtyard building overlooking the River Thames in central London. The buildings have housed a variety of bodies, including government departments and educational societies. More recently, arts and cultural events have taken centre stage. In the last ten years the courtyard has been the venue for a regular outdoor cinema, iceskating, fashion shows, and rock and dance events.

*What events would you propose staging in the courtyard, and what facilities would you need to support these activities?*

# Public toilets

serve a very important function for the citizens of any city. Generally they are pretty ugly, but they don't have to be. The two examples shown here are sculptural and more like art installations set in the environment of a public park.

*Jinhua Architecture Park, China.*
*DnA Design and Architecture, 2004.*

*Trail Restroom, Austin, Texas, USA.*
*Miró Rivera Architects, 2007.*

*Design your own public toilets while considering*
*light, ventilation and appearance.*

The **threshold** of a building – its entrance – can be envisaged as the portal between the public realm of the street and the private world of the interior. Most entrances are fairly anonymous and don't really say anything about the people, events and functions inside. The two entrances shown here suggest a narrative beyond the threshold.

*Binoculars Building (former Chiat\Day Building), Los Angeles, California, USA. Claes Oldenburg/ Coosje van Bruggen and Frank O. Gehry, 1991.*

*Le Cabaret de l'Enfer, Paris, France, 1898.*

*Design an entrance for a building with one of the following functions: pet shop, recycling centre, chocolate factory.*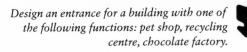

When walking through a city we often experience our journey through a **series of framed views** containing places, objects, events, spaces and people. The drawn sequence can be made into a storyboard and is often how film-makers envisage the backdrop to a scene within a movie. My drawings take a walk around the area of St Paul's Cathedral, London. Note that each frame has at least some part of the previous image within it to connect the story together.

*Storyboard a journey through your city and be careful to connect each frame.*

Man's desire to develop **underwater cities** has in recent years resulted in a number of designers exploring the concept of the 'seascraper'. In this version below, the Malaysian architect Sarly Adre Sarkum envisages a self-sufficient structure that generates its own electricity using solar, wind and wave power. It utilizes its own food-farming system and sustains a small forest on the surface of the vessel. The 'Water-Scraper' is kept upright using a system of ballasts aided by squid-like tentacles that generate kinetic energy.

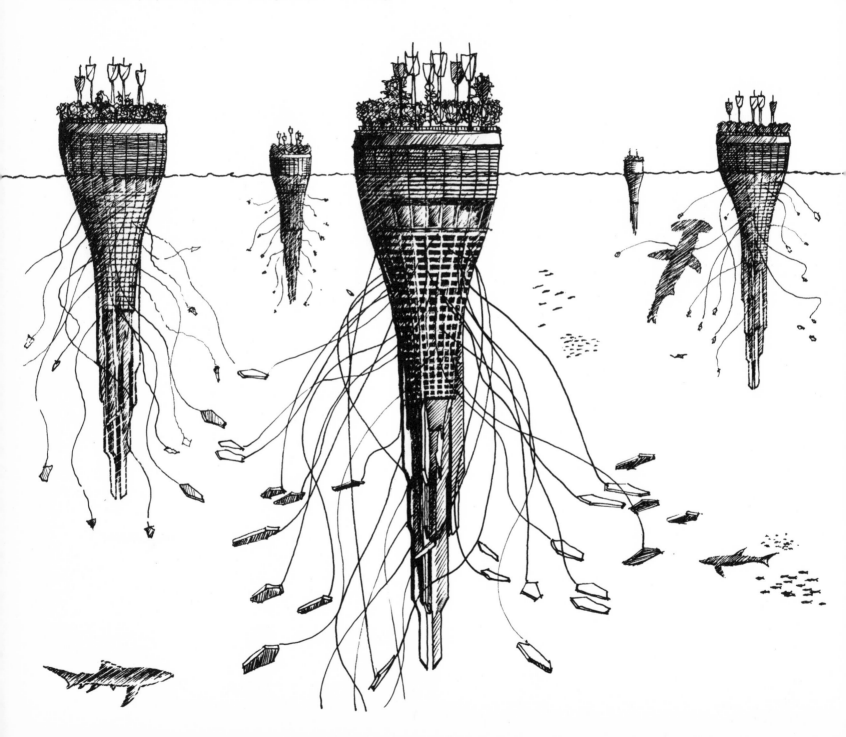

*Design your own self-sustaining seascraper. Think how you might generate and harvest energy, and provide food and areas to live, work and play.*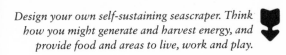

The **Gavina Showroom** in Bologna, Italy, by Carlo Scarpa (1961–1963) is an example of a storefront that defines and frames the display of merchandise using strong geometry, a palette of raw materials such as board-marked concrete, and a Japanese-inspired gate.

*Design your own showroom, using abstract geometry, to display modern artworks.* ▶▶

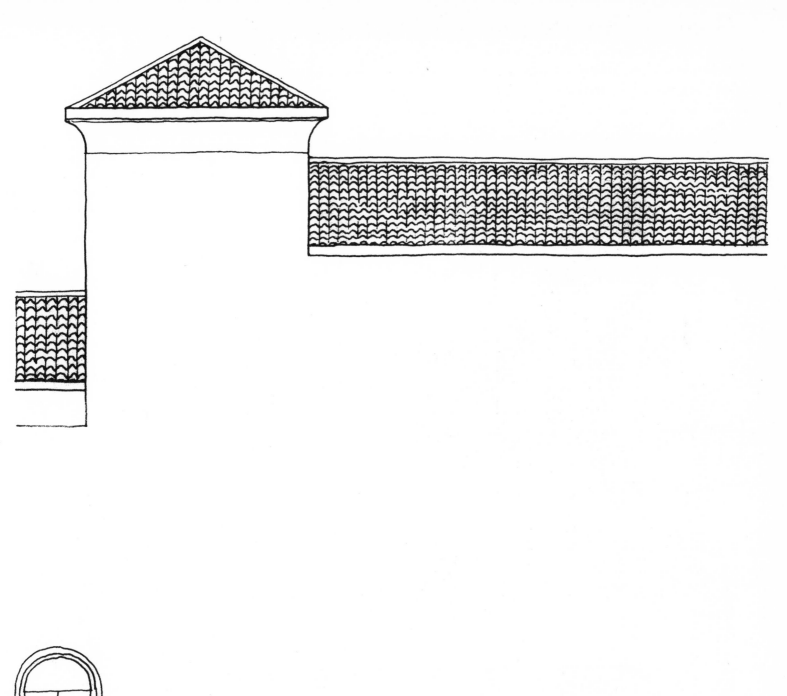

Below is an example of one of the very earliest forms of **natural ventilation** in the city of Hyderabad, founded in 1768 by Mian Ghulam Shah Kalhoro in Pakistan's Sind province. The triangular towers are almost like chimneys on top of the dwellings and are used to funnel cool breezes into the interior. You can also see BedZED, a modern example designed by architect Bill Dunster for environmentally friendly housing on the edge of London in 2002 (below right).

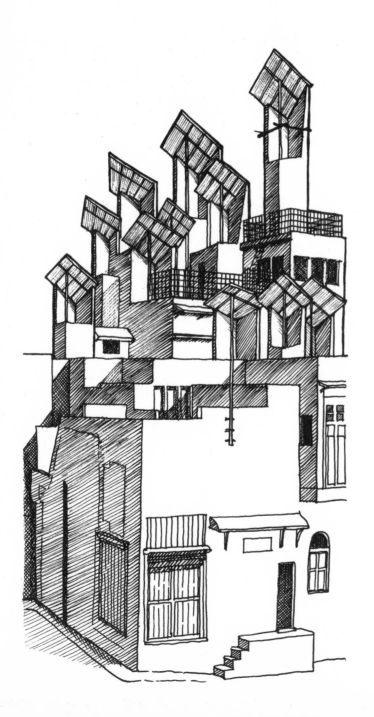

*Sketch a series of ideas for windcatchers on these traditional roofs and consider if they rotate and what they are made of.*

Many cities have a **monument or statue** that symbolizes the freedom or the protection of its people. Rio de Janeiro has a statue of Christ the Redeemer, New York has the Statue of Liberty, and Giza, Egypt, has the Great Sphinx. What does your nearest city have?

*Design a statue that you think would be a symbol of protection or freedom for citizens.*

While researching different **bus shelters,** I came across some that exemplified a cultural character and thought it would be interesting to design a bus shelter dedicated to a particular place or city.

*Left: Lavaca bus shelter, San Antonio, Texas, USA. Carlos Cortes, 2005. Commissioned by the Office of Cultural Affairs.*
*Below left: Taraz bus shelter, Kazakhstan, architect unknown.*
*Below: 'Cascade' bus shelter, Orlando, Florida, USA. John Marhoefer/Walt Geiger, 2012.*

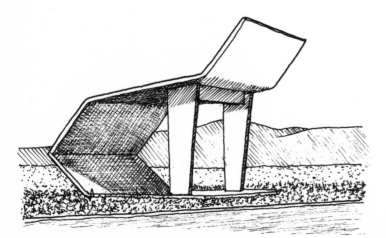

*Sketch your version on this street scene.*

# Street lighting is a very important part of any city, helping to make spaces safe at night.

In recent years street lighting has been developed that mimics how plants open to collect the sun's energy. This example, designed by Philips, opens up and collects solar energy during the day and then closes and emits light at night, but only when people are in close proximity.

*Sketch your own ideas for sustainable street lighting and think about ways of creating renewable energy within its design ...*

Here are some more **city silhouettes.** Try to identify them and then make a new hybrid silhouette using features from each city.

*Combine these cities, or try incorporating landmarks from your favourite cities.*

These are copies of the visionary drawings by **Iakov Chernikhov,** the Russian
Constructivist architect, completed between 1927 and 1933. He used line, block and plane to express the
machine-like quality of his compositions.

*Extend this composition in perspective and add
your own extension to his city.*

These two examples of Chernikhov's work only use the medium of **line and grid.**

*Draw two more using just geometric lines and frames.*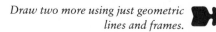

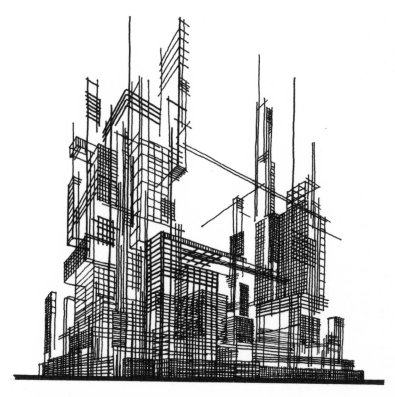

These **tram stations** in Hannover, Germany, were designed by Despang Architekten for Expo 2000. While the framework and geometry remain the same throughout the series, the materials used for each individual stop vary, chosen to reflect their local surroundings and local history.

*Create your own series of shelters using a structure that could evolve its appearance in some way.*

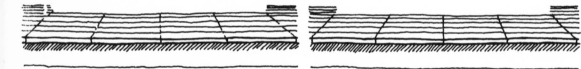

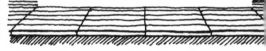

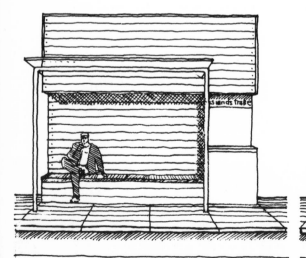

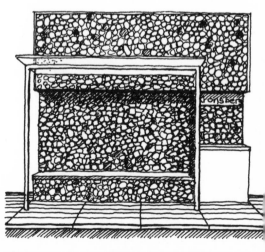

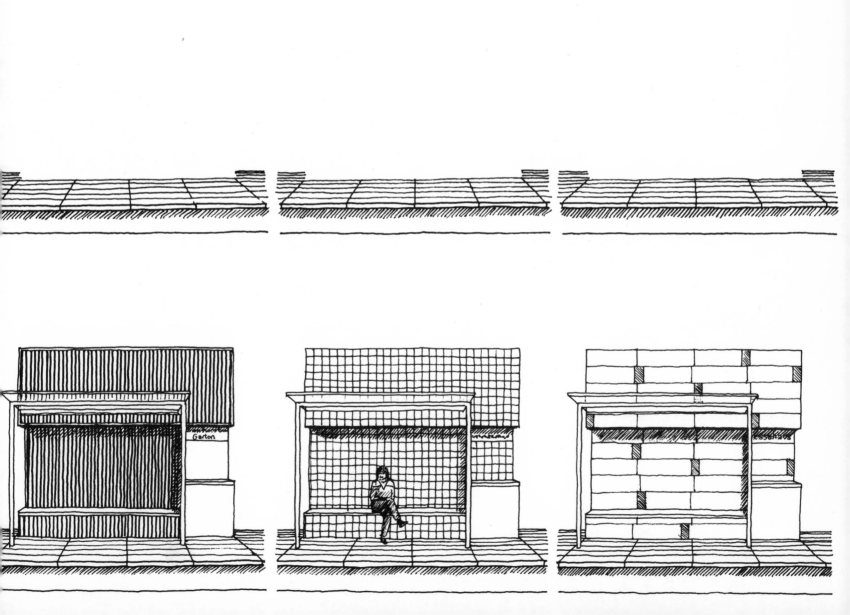

Here is a drawing of the space occupied by **Central Park** in New York City. Design a new park for the twenty-first century, considering the kinds of activities, events and facilities that would engage and enhance the lives of New Yorkers. Would they want sports or art activities? Or maybe a contrast to the city itself, such as nature and wildlife?

*Create your own park in the space provided.*

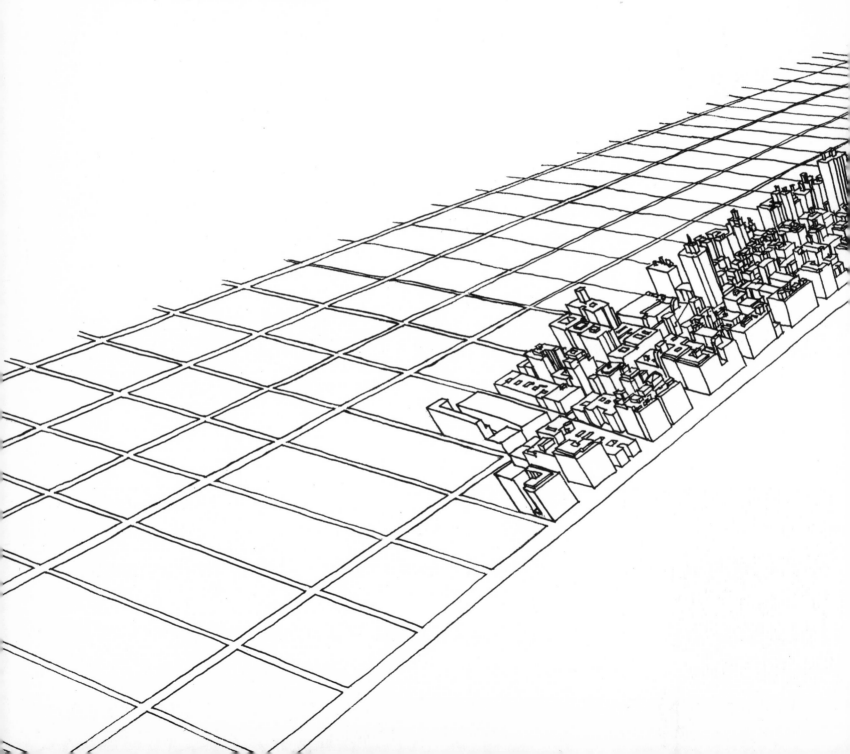

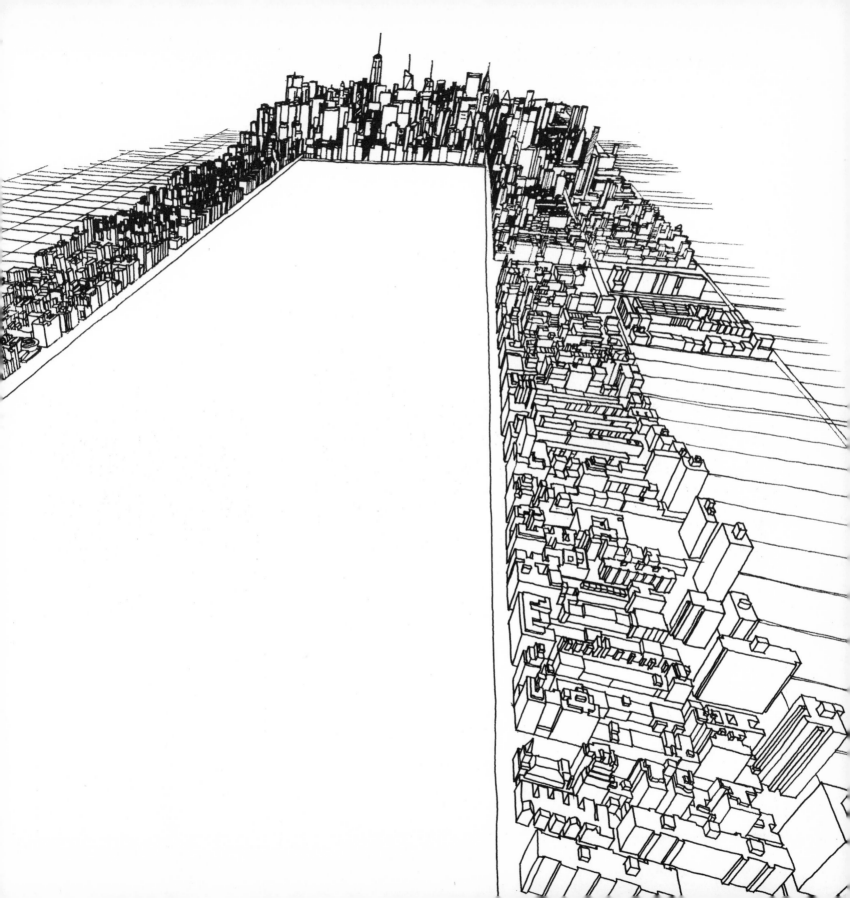

In his book **'Image of the City'** (1960) urban planner Kevin Lynch put forward the idea that cities could be defined using five key elements: paths, edges, districts, nodes and landmarks. To illustrate these concepts I have drawn examples of where these elements can be found in a variety of major cities: London, New York, San Francisco and Barcelona.

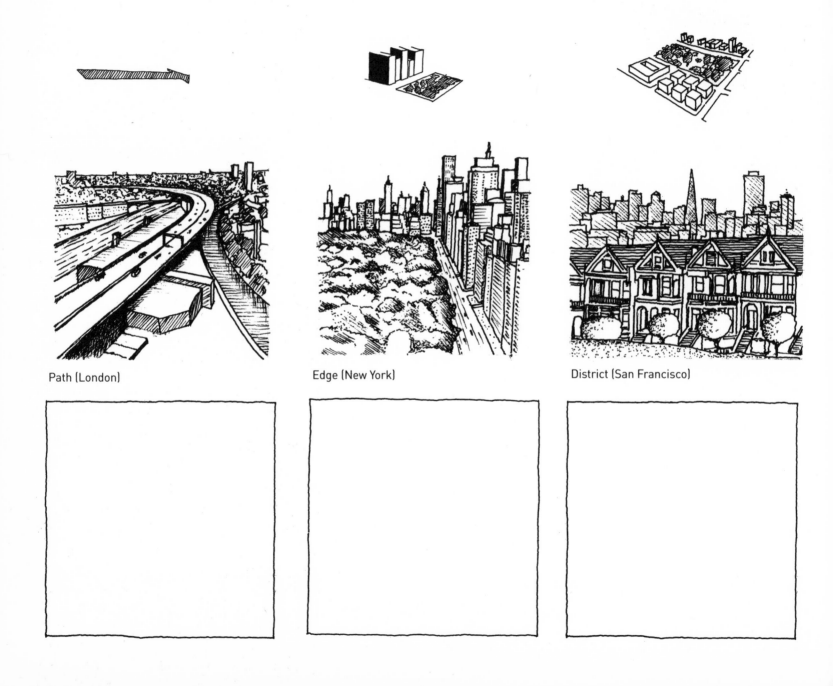

Path (London)

Edge (New York)

District (San Francisco)

*Walk around your nearest city and sketch examples of a path, an edge, a district, a node and a landmark.*

Node (London)

Landmark (Barcelona)

Bulgarian artist Christo and Moroccan-born Jeanne-Claude are famous for **wrapping buildings**
and landscapes. In 1995 they wrapped the German parliament building (the Reichstag) in Berlin in 100,000 square metres
(1.1 million square feet) of fireproof polypropylene and aluminium fabric. The effect was simply stunning.

*Using this sketch of the Arc du Triomphe in Paris as*
*a starting point, add your own wrapping.*

In the 1960s the celebrated avant-garde architectural group **Archigram** challenged conventional ideas about living in cities. The six members of the group designed and contributed design projects in the form of a magazine using pop-art drawings and graphics as a way of exposing their ideas about the future of urban culture. They devised 'Walking Cities', 'Plug-in Cities', and this, my rendering of the nomadic 'Living Pod' (1965–66) by David Greene. Amazingly, these ideas about the relationship between cities and future technology are now 50 years old.

*What kind of living pod would you propose, and how would current technology influence the design?*

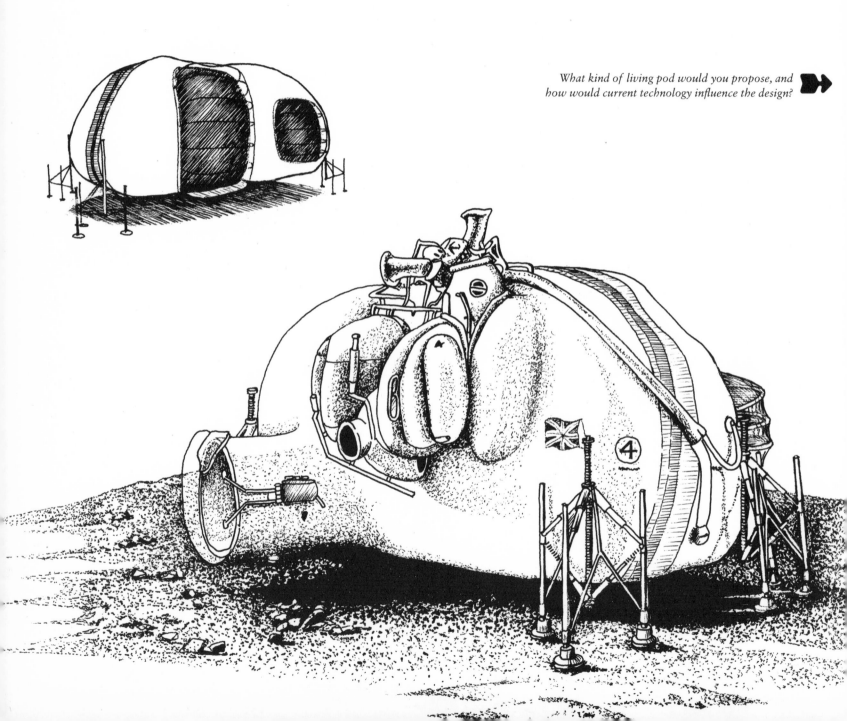

The **shopping arcade** became popular in European cities in the eighteenth and nineteenth centuries and was the predecessor of the North American shopping mall. The arcade provided a safe, pedestrian-only, covered internal street that would provide comfort regardless of climatic and social conditions.

*Design your own arcade. Consider the profile and structure and how the passage is lit. What type of shops and cafes would you include?*

*The Burlington Arcade, London. Samuel Ware, 1819.*

Most **superstore design** is boring. In 1974, the Best Products company challenged this notion by commissioning the Sculpture in the Environment (SITE) architects to design a series of nine buildings across the USA that would re-brand their company. SITE's idea was to take the building envelope and break it down via a series of distortions, fragmentations and displacements.

*Notch Showroom, Miami, Florida.*
*SITE, 1979.*

*Peeling Project Showroom, Richmond, Virginia. SITE, 1972.*

*Tilt Showroom, Towson, Maryland. SITE, 1976.*

*Given a simple box as a starting point, how would you make your superstore distinctive?*

Images of the city have played an important role in many **film, theatre and music** performances. The example below, influenced by the film *Metropolis* by Fritz Lang (1927) was the design of the stage set for David Bowie's 'Diamond Dogs' tour in 1974.

*Design your own stage set based on an image of the city for either a play, musical or rock act.*

*Stage set for 'Diamond Dogs', designed by Jules Fisher and Mark Ravitz, 1974.*

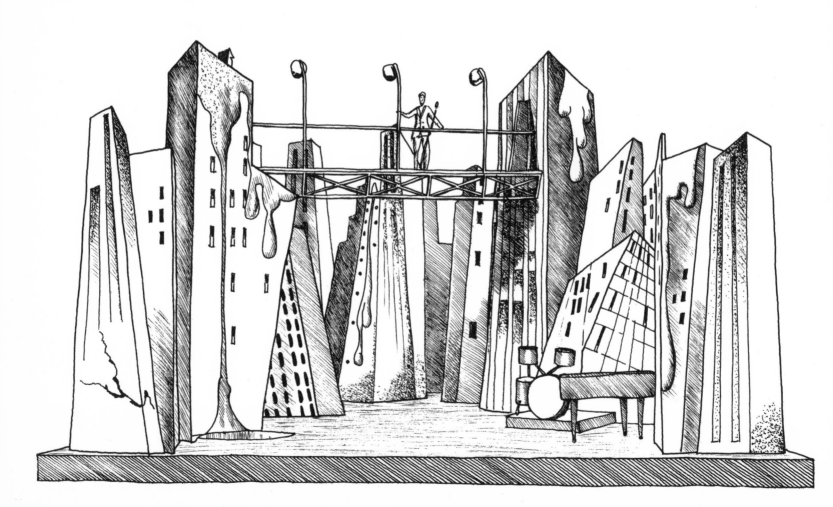

The district of Akihabara, Tokyo, is known as **'Electric Town'** because of its shops dedicated to electronic goods and its array of neon signage. Below is a typical street showing signage, advertising and lighting, and on the opposite page is the same street without any signs.

*Colour in the image below and invent your own electric town on the right.*

# Roosevelt Island

is a narrow island in New York's East River, which has been the site of numerous architectural competitions over the years. One particular competition entry, from the German architect O.M. Ungers in 1975, imagined the city development as a series of blocks formed from different typologies, such as towers, courtyards and terraces.

*What other variations can you devise on the Ungers blocks shown here?*

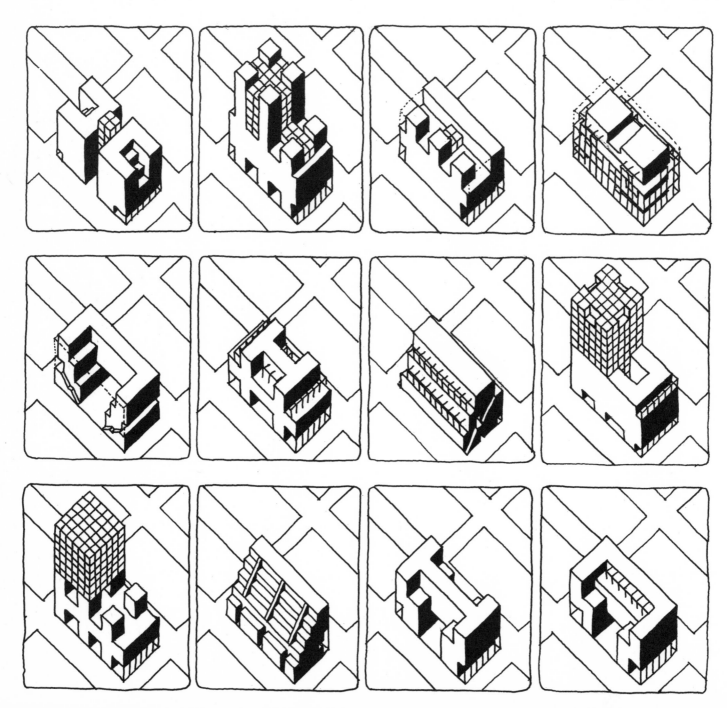

The corners and junctions of streets are often celebrated by important **landmark buildings.**
The Lois & Richard Rosenthal Center for Contemporary Art, Cincinnati, USA, by Zaha Hadid Architects (2003) deals with the variety of conflicting scales of the surrounding buildings by using a variety of horizontal forms.

*Given the same situation, what 3D forms, structure and scale would you use to create a successful corner building?*

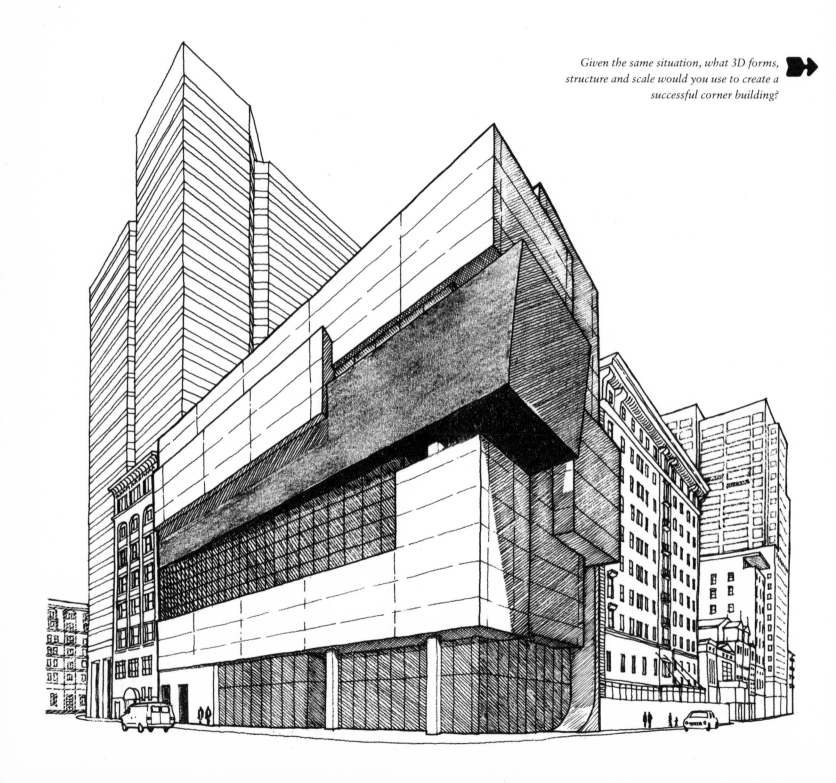

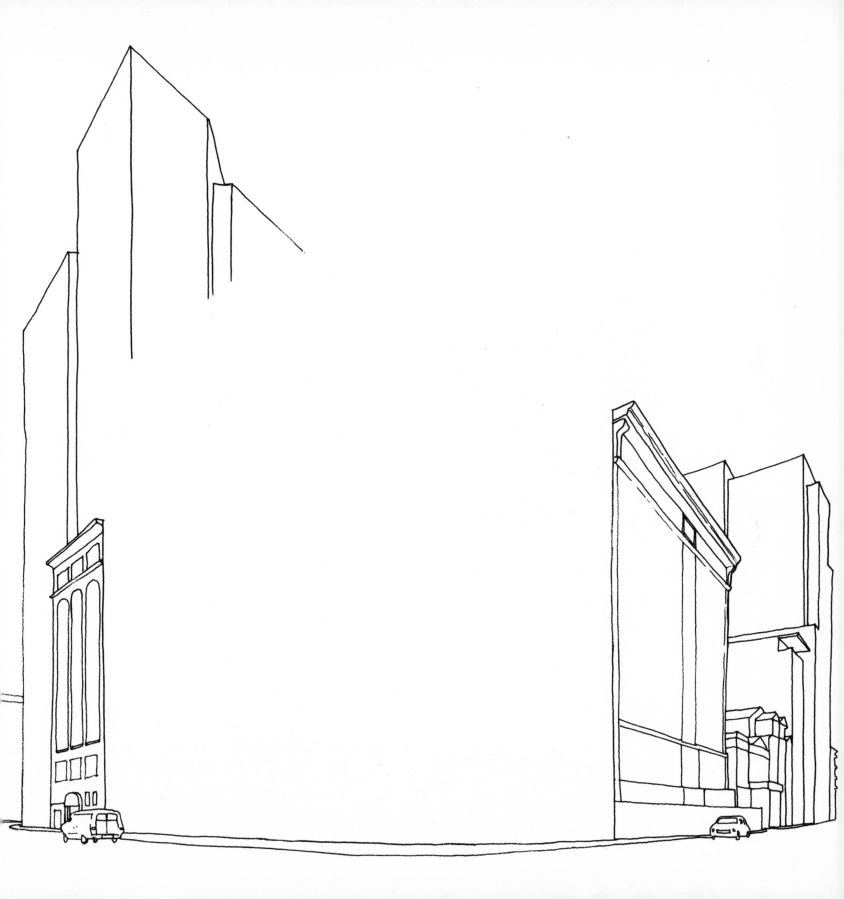

Famed for inventing the geodesic dome, US architect, engineer and inventor **Buckminster Fuller**
proposed putting a vast dome over the whole of Manhattan Island, New York. He also calculated that given the right atmospheric
conditions, such as in the heat of the desert, his geodesic sphere would float because the heated air within the structural tubes
would be lighter than the surrounding ambient temperature.

*Imagine a whole floating city in one of Fuller's geodesic
structures and sketch it in the space provided.*

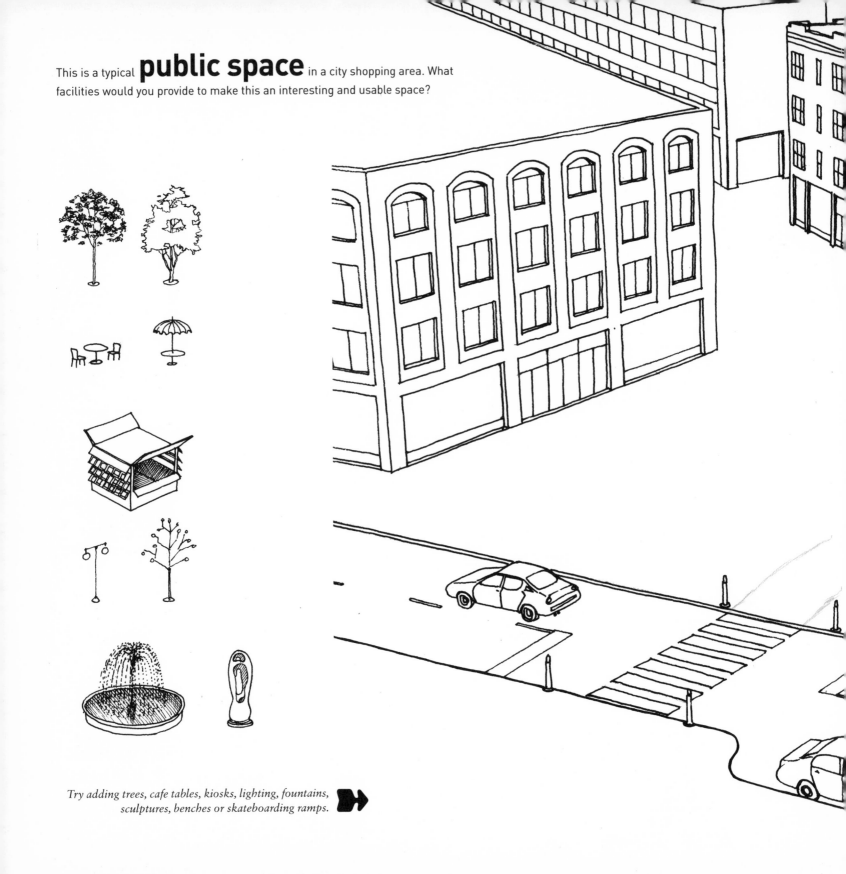

This is a typical **public space** in a city shopping area. What facilities would you provide to make this an interesting and usable space?

*Try adding trees, cafe tables, kiosks, lighting, fountains, sculptures, benches or skateboarding ramps.*

In 2011 a competition to design a new **metro entrance** in the centre of the city
was launched in San Sebastián, northern Spain. These examples from architects Snøhetta (first prize) and
BABELstudio show different approaches to shelter, threshold and materials.

*Sketch out your own ideas for a new metro stop
and consider the surrounding streetscape.* ➤➤

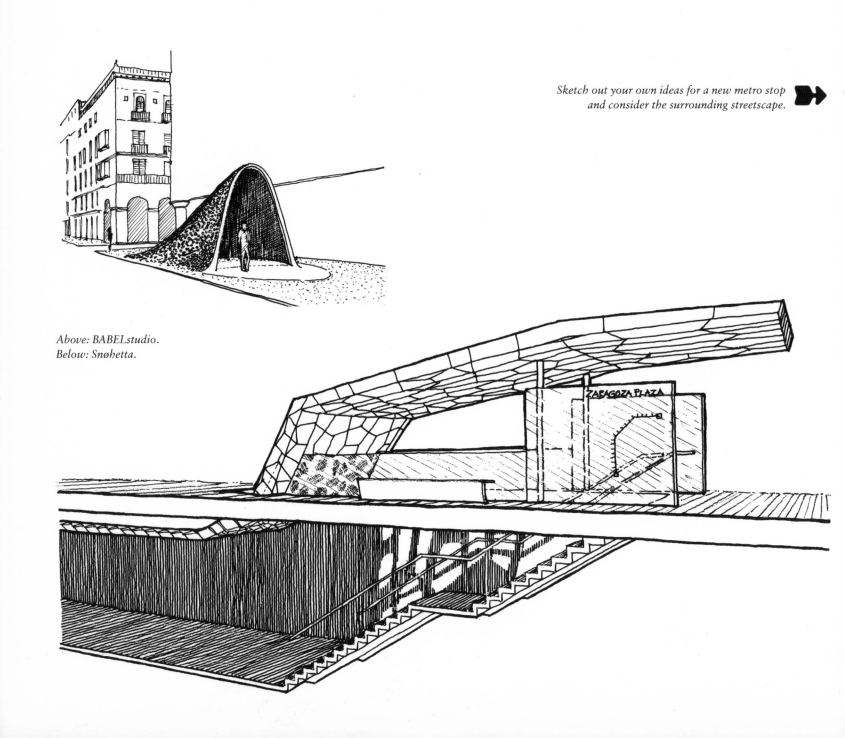

*Above: BABELstudio.*
*Below: Snøhetta.*

ZARAGOZA PLAZA

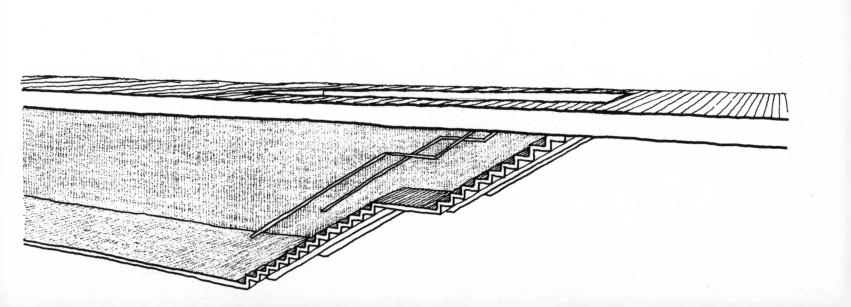

# High-density urban areas characterize

many Mediterranean towns and cities, with people living in buildings tightly packed together. Issues such as privacy, noise, light, views and outside space are a major concern for the inhabitants. Preserving the basic form of the buildings, how would you alter their relationship to each other?

Suggest new types of windows and balconies, extensions and different materials – maybe even bridges between houses.

In her designs for a series of buildings for the **Sugamo Shinkin Bank**
in Tokyo, the French-born architect Emmanuelle Moureaux challenged the image of the bank as a building
that is predominantly formal and staid. Her clever use of geometry, massing, colour and manipulation of window
openings offered a new freedom to a building type traditionally known for its sombre appearance.

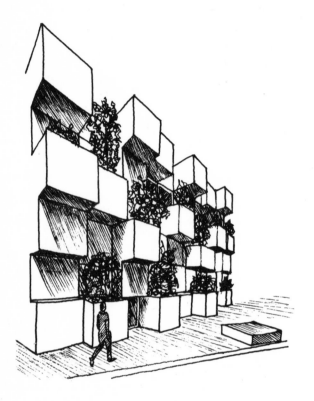

*Sugamo Shinkin Bank, Nakaaoki branch, Tokyo, 2014.*

*Sugamo Shinkin Bank, Shimura branch, Tokyo, 2013.*

*Sugamo Shinkin Bank, Tokiwadai branch, Tokyo, 2010.*

*Sketch ideas for other institutions that are in need of a twenty-first-century makeover. Maybe start with your local bank.*

In 1922 the American architect Hugh Ferriss made a series of drawings detailing **'the cutback principle'.** These demonstrated how skyscrapers in major American cities could be modelled to allow light into the surrounding streets. The cutback principle had formed the basis for zoning laws introduced in 1916, and Ferriss illustrated what high-rise structures might look like based on this idea.

*Using this partly modelled block as a starting point, form your own skyscraper using this principle.*

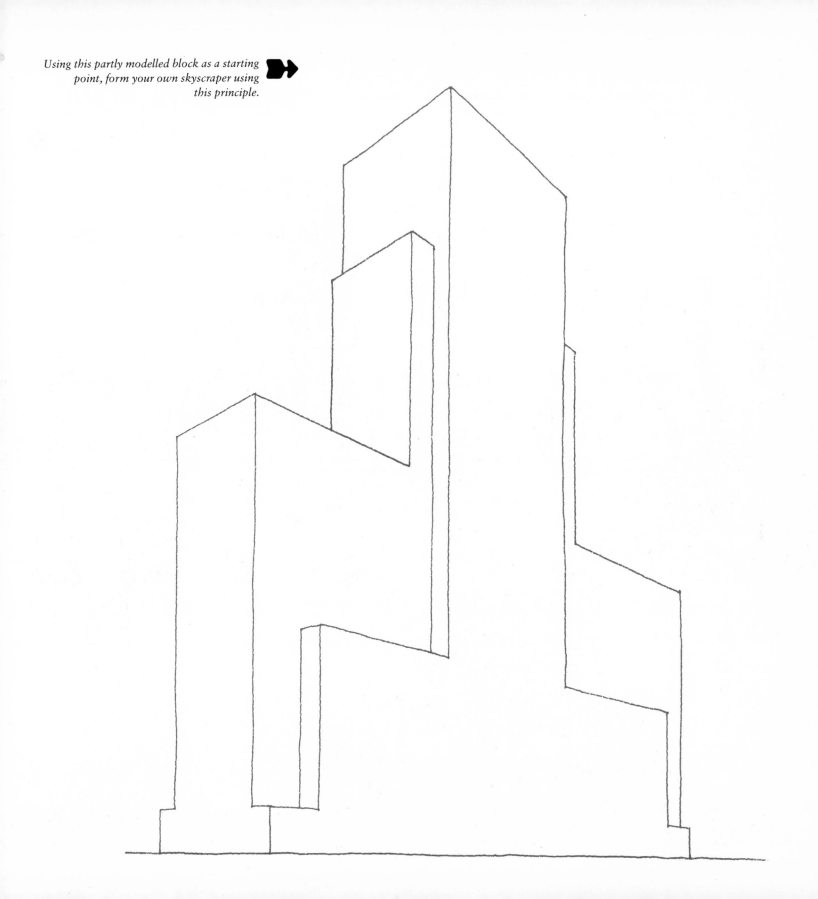

Entitled 'Very Large Structure', this project for a **nomadic city** is the vision of Spanish architect Manuel Domínguez. Similar to Ron Herron's (Archigram) 'Walking City', VLS moves on massive caterpillar tracks across desert terrains. Add your own city to this partially completed drawing.

*Consider what kind of buildings would be needed to sustain life in a hostile environment.*

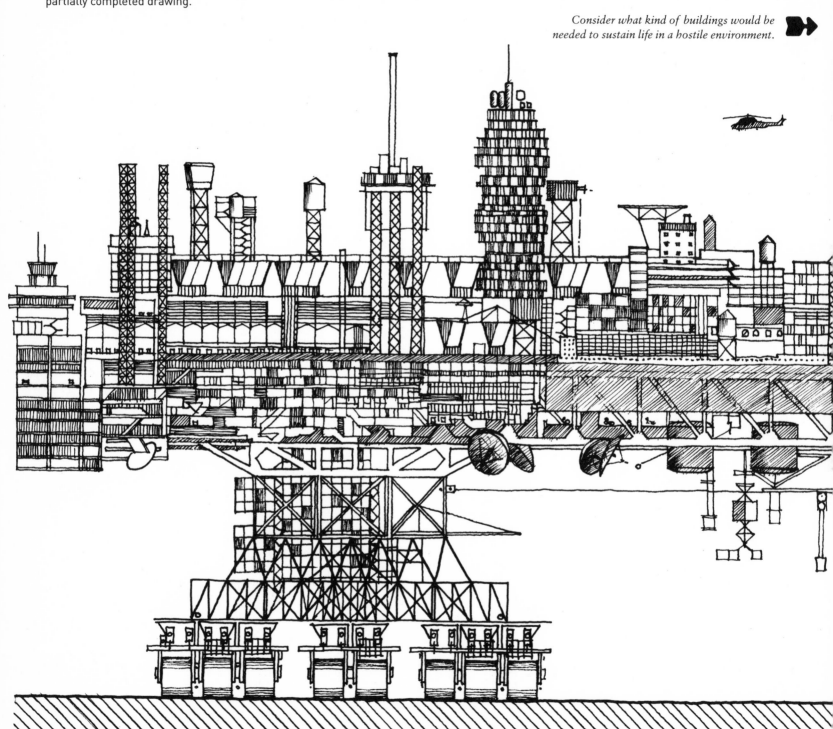

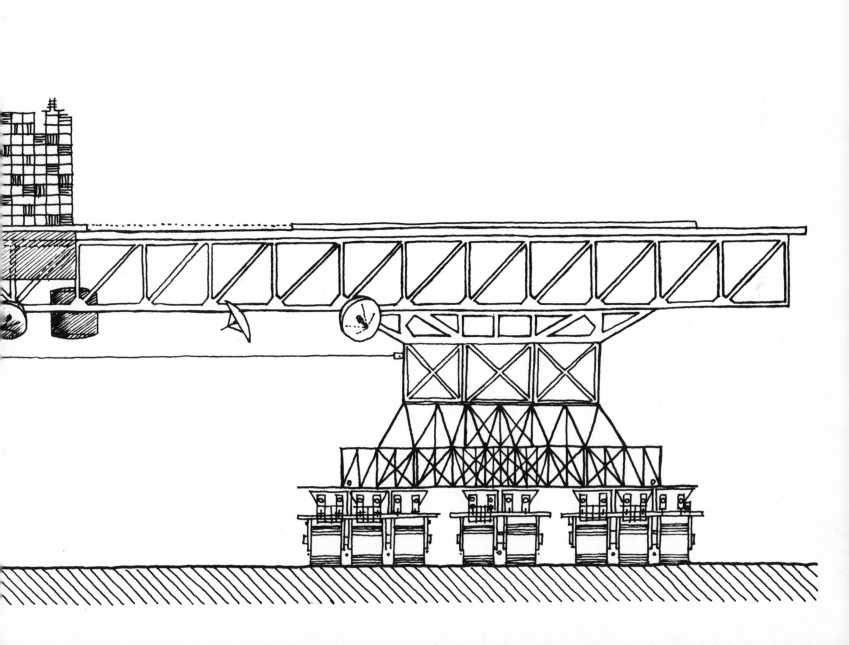

# Airport buildings

**Airport buildings** are often the first and
last memory that one has of a city when visiting a foreign country.
The TWA terminal at JFK International Airport, New York, was
designed by Eero Saarinen and Associates in 1962 and was based
on the idea of a large bird either landing or about to take off.

*Sketch some ideas for an airport for your nearest city.
What characterizes it, and does it relate to the national
identity, culture or location?*

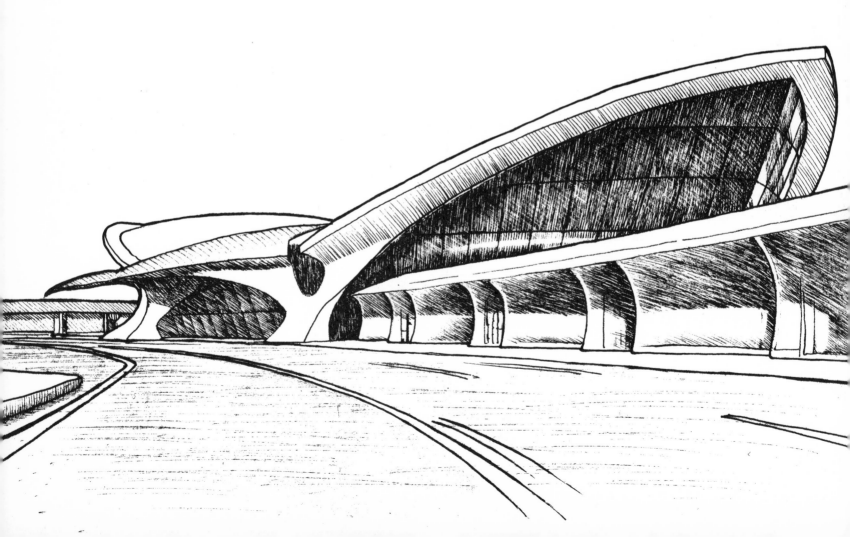

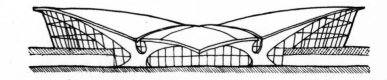

This **maze** is a partially completed design for a labyrinthine city. One side faces the ocean and the other side faces the forest. Imagine that you have arrived by boat and have to negotiate a path through the city to reach your destination in the forest.

*Colour and complete the drawing, adding houses and gardens.* ▶▶

In the 1950s and 1960s at **service stations** on the Italian Autostrade, the Pavesi Autogrill restaurants celebrated the luxury of travelling by car by constructing heroic bridge buildings spanning the roads. Their customers could relax while enjoying the latest automobile fashion parade.

*Design a bridge building in the same spirit as the Italian examples.*

*Pavesi Autogrill Restaurant, Montepulciano, Italy. Angelo Bianchetti, 1967.*

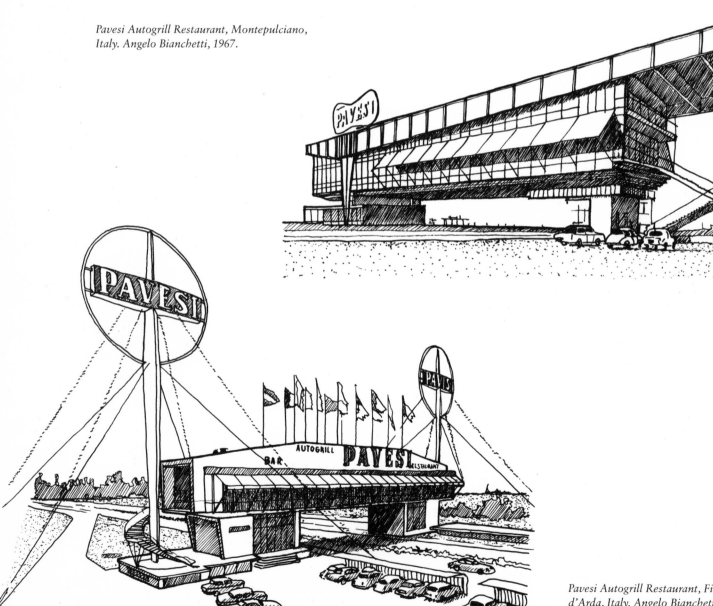

*Pavesi Autogrill Restaurant, Fiorenzuola d'Arda, Italy. Angelo Bianchetti, 1959.*

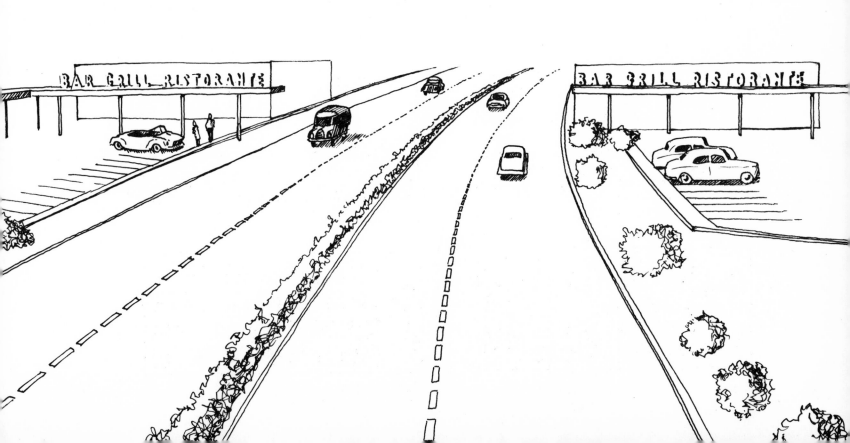

These **housing typology diagrams** were taken from one of my old sketchbooks and compare how one might organize arrangements for types of housing in the city. The generic types are terraces, courtyards, blocks, towers and villas, with each one a variation on the next.

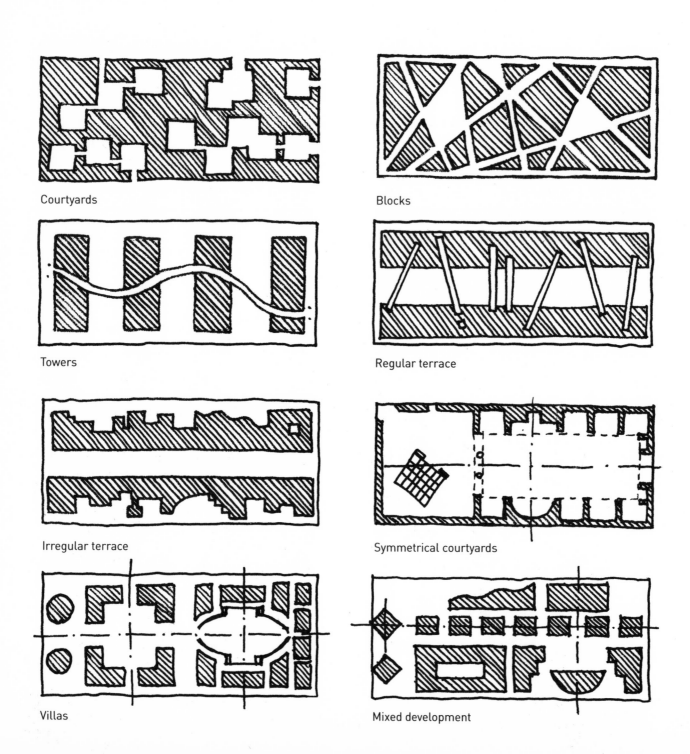

Courtyards

Blocks

Towers

Regular terrace

Irregular terrace

Symmetrical courtyards

Villas

Mixed development

*Draw your own versions, considering scale and proportion, and the allocation of space and light to the street and gardens.*

# Gas stations

are one type of building that appears in almost every city and yet does not feature in many architectural journals. Often viewed as a piece of background architecture with functional design ambitions, the gas station has occasionally given rise to some expressive structures. The ones illustrated have become landmarks within the urban landscape.

*'Auto Palace' gas station, Muldersweg, Nijmegen, the Netherlands. B.J. Meerman and Johan van der Pijll, 1936.*

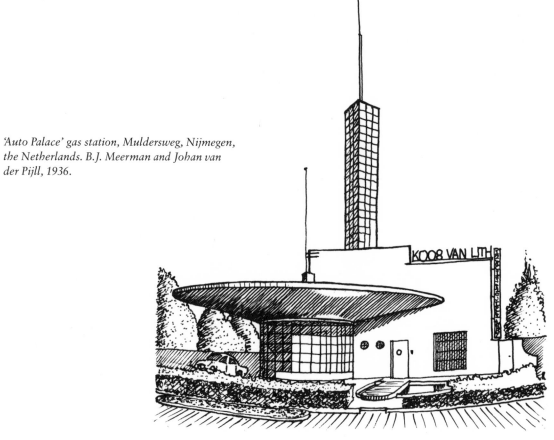

*Enco gas station, Palm Springs, California, USA. Albert Frey and Robson C. Chambers, 1965.*

*Sketch out some ideas for a service station that could become a feature in your nearest city.*

*NP gas station, Madrid, Spain. Moneo-Brock, 2007.*

In his 1910 essay 'Ornament and Crime' the Austrian architect **Adolph Loos** put forward the idea that superfluous decoration on buildings was akin to a criminal act. Loos' design for the Müller House predicated the Modernist, Functionalist and, more recently, Minimalist movements of the 20th century, which had a huge impact on the appearance of our cities. More recently, though, digital manufacturing techniques have resulted in buildings becoming more decorative again. How might this change the appearance of the Müller House?

Create a 'crime' of your own by
decorating the Müller House.

# The Dynamic Tower, also known as the Da Vinci Tower, is a proposal for a

mixed-use moving skyscraper designed by architect David Fisher for Dubai. Each floor rotates independently around a fixed core and it is proposed that the whole building will be powered by wind turbines and solar panels, with the major components being prefabricated off site.

*If you were to design a kinetic skyscraper, what would it look like? Consider how you might harvest energy to power its movement.*

The **Nolli Plan** of Rome was surveyed and drawn between 1736 and 1748 by the Italian architect Giambattista Nolli (sometimes known as Giovanni Battista). His maps are significant because they describe the interiors of public buildings as if they were exterior spaces like streets and squares – in other words, public spaces. On the right-hand page I have erased a section of this map for you to complete.

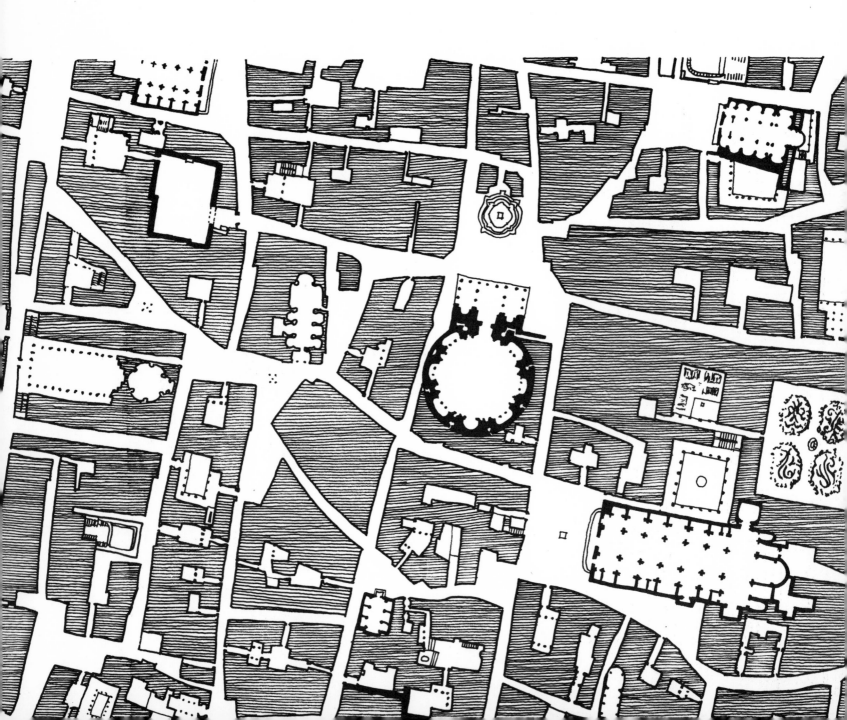

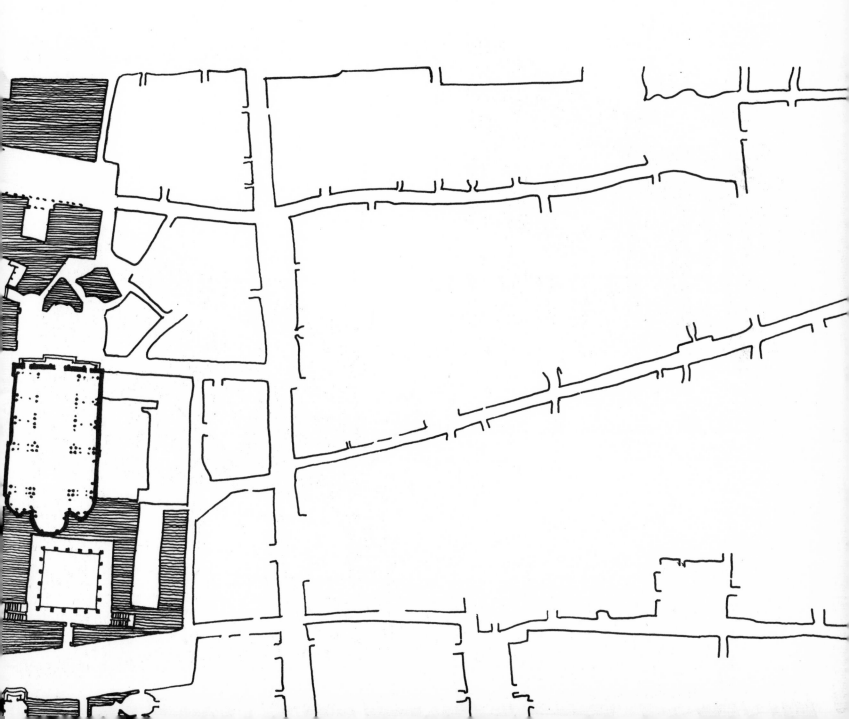

*Draw courtyards, squares, streets, arcades, libraries, churches, mosques, parks and gardens.*

# Here we can see **artists interacting with architecture.**

The first artist attached an inflated bubble containing a palm tree and hammock to a museum; the second cut an eight-metre- (six-foot-) diameter disc into the facade of a local building and attached it to a motor, turning this section of the building inside out in a cycle lasting just over two minutes.

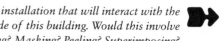

*Propose an installation that will interact with the outside and inside of this building. Would this involve cutting? Masking? Peeling? Superimposing?*

'Klimakapsel Oase Nr. 7' (Climate Capsule, Oasis No. 7), Museum of the Arts and Crafts, Hamburg Germany. Haus-Rucker-Co, 1972.

'Turning the Place Over', Liverpool Biennial. Richard Wilson, 2007.

# The proportions of a street – the general building height compared
to the width – will determine how much daylight illuminates the space. This will invariably affect the mood of the
place. As you can see from these sectional street diagrams, the proportion is determined by height to width and
is measured in imaginary squares (ratios such as 1:1, 1:2, 1:3 or even 1:1.5).

1:2 or 1:3

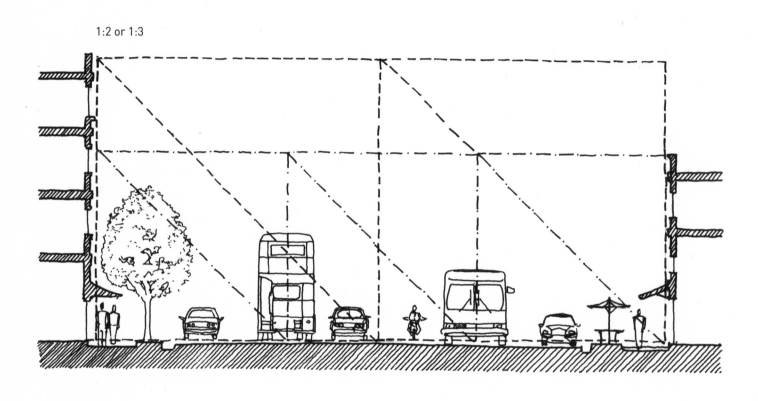

1:1.5

1:1

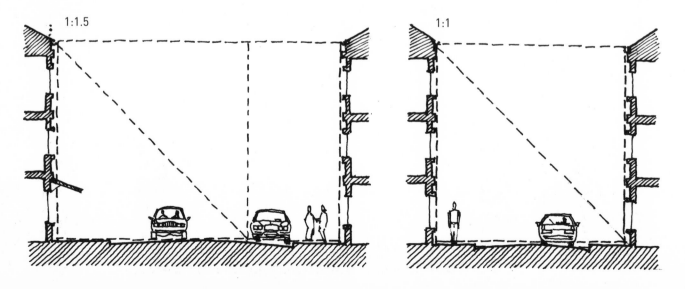

*Sketch the outline of your street and try to establish the proportions.*

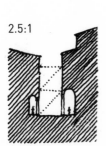

2.5:1

1:3

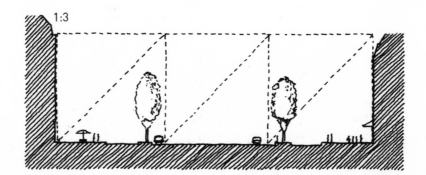

6:1

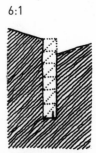

The centre of London has many beautiful **public squares** but the gardens in the centre of them are often private. The example shown is Bedford Square in Bloomsbury, London.

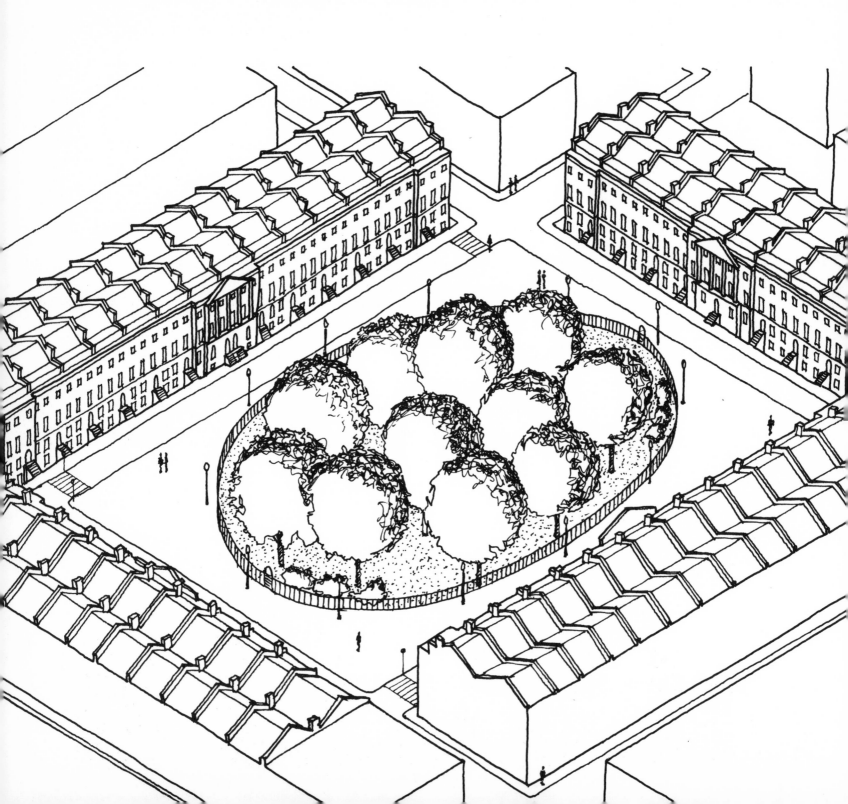

*Imagine if the central garden was made public. Would you keep the garden or propose a different landscape? Who would use it — office workers, shoppers, children?*

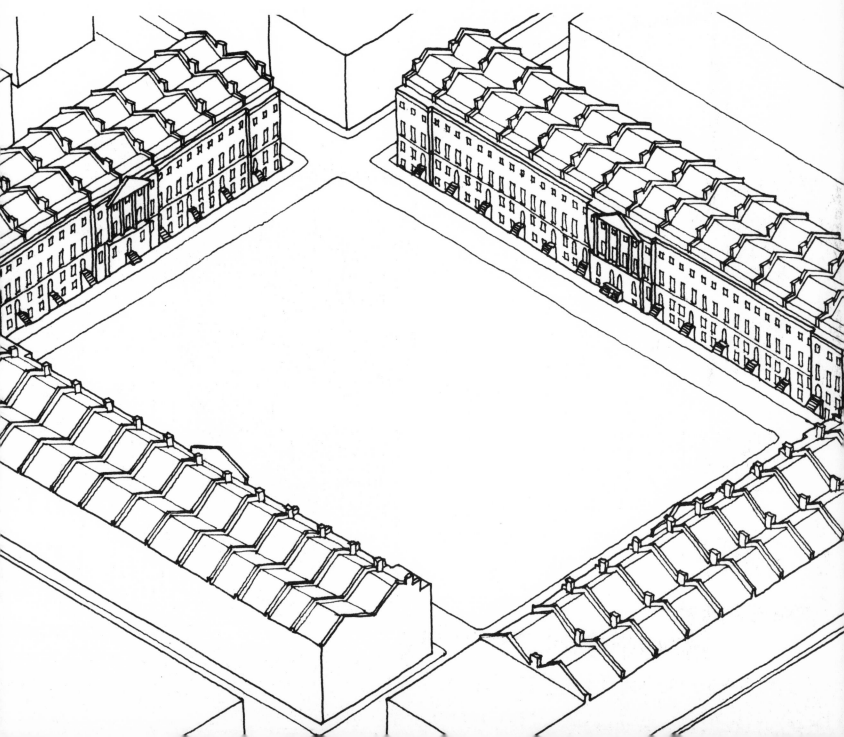

Running through the centre of **medieval Girona** in northern Spain is the Onya River, which is bound by houses and apartments that are typical of a Mediterranean city. The facades are painted in rich earth colours according to a palette created by Enric Ansesa, James J. Faixó, and the architects Josep Fuses and Joan Maria Viader.

*Design new facades for the missing buildings and suggest your own palette for all of the buildings.*

These four examples of **gateways** to a city are largely symbolic as they constitute not only a landmark in the city, but also often relate to a particular historic event invoking ideals such as peace, freedom, liberty, protection and commemoration.

*Gateway Arch, St Louis, USA. Eero Saarinen, 1965.*

*Brandenburg Gate, Berlin. Carl Gotthard Langhans, 1791.*

*India Gate, Delhi. Edwin Lutyens, 1931.*

*Heian-jingu Shrine, Torii Gate, Kyoto, Japan. Ito Chuta, 1895.*

Design your own city gateway. Maybe it relates to a particular event in history, or maybe it is designed using modern forms and materials.

# 'What is the city but the people?'

asked William Shakespeare, implying that the character of a place is formed by its citizens. These silhouettes of city dwellers represent some of the typical sorts of people who use public spaces and facilities. Along the foot of the page are icons that denote some of their daily requirements.

*City dwellers: Skateboarder, elderly person, young family, busker.*

*Icons (top row) nature, hard surface, shelter, washing facilities, drinking water, toilet facilities, tables, relaxing, space to sleep.*
*(bottom row) populated space, unpopulated space, noisy space, quiet space, cycling.*

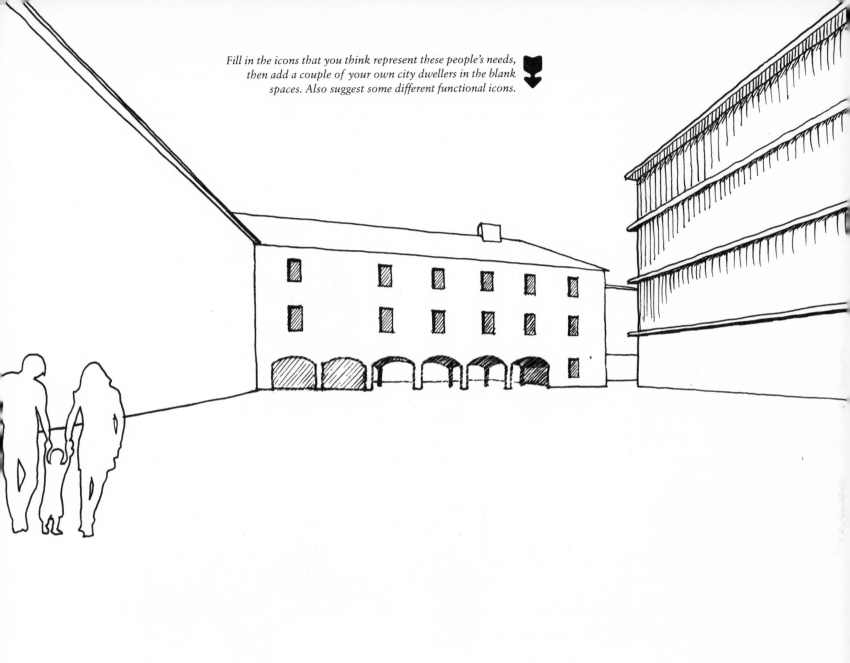

Fill in the icons that you think represent these people's needs, then add a couple of your own city dwellers in the blank spaces. Also suggest some different functional icons.

Many cities have a permanent theme park and funfair. **Coney Island** in Brooklyn developed as an amusement area in the late 1800s, and soon became one of the most popular theme parks in the USA. One of its main attractions was the 'Elephantine Colossus', built as a 34-room hotel in 1885. At 46 metres (150 feet) tall, the Colossus was so large that at one time it was the first thing that visitors would see upon arriving in New York. Unfortunately it was destroyed by fire in 1896 and only photographs and drawings now exist of this amazing structure.

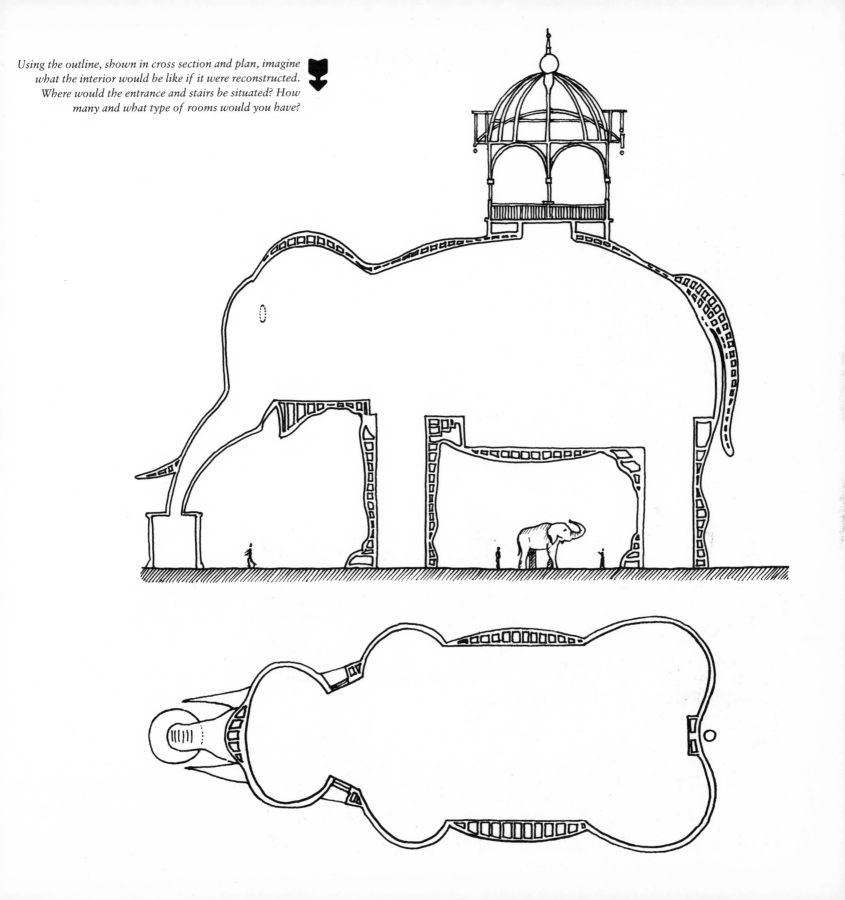

*Using the outline, shown in cross section and plan, imagine what the interior would be like if it were reconstructed. Where would the entrance and stairs be situated? How many and what type of rooms would you have?*

In 1922, famous Swiss-born architect Le Corbusier proposed a **'Contemporary City'** for three million inhabitants in response to the growing problem of the Paris slums. His 'Plan Voisin' (1925) envisaged the removal of two square miles of downtown Paris to provide a new housing quarter set within a large parkland.

*What would you propose putting in this cleared area of Paris?*

*Sketch showing model and plan of the proposed business district and part of the residential, cultural and governmental district extending west along the Seine.*

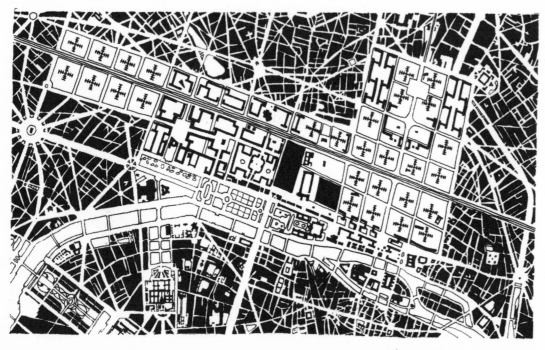

These two buildings are examples of **museums** that have been dedicated to a single artist. Dalí said of The Salvador Dalí Theatre-Museum that 'I want my museum to be a single block, a labyrinth, a great surrealist object … the people who come to see it will leave with the sensation of having had a theatrical dream'. The other example is dedicated to the Swiss painter Paul Klee and, while abstract in form, has a connection with Klee's famous quote that 'drawing is taking a line for a walk'.

*Zentrum Paul Klee, Bern, Switzerland.*
*Renzo Piano, 2005.*

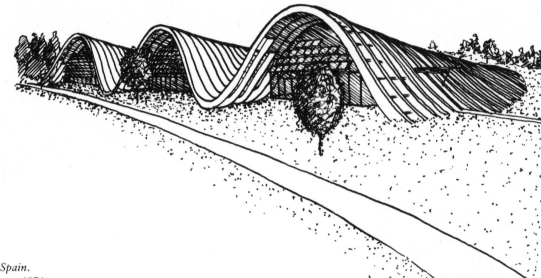

*The Salvador Dalí Theatre-Museum, Figueres, Spain.*
*Joaquim de Ros i Ramis and Alexandre Bonaterra, 1974.*

*Choose your favourite artist and sketch what their museum might look like. Consider colour, form and materials, as well as what the artist was passionate about.*

Many city skylines are characterized by the **roofs and towers** of their important religious and civic buildings. The Cathedral of Vasily the Blessed, better known as Saint Basil's Cathedral, in Moscow's Red Square has become both a focal point and a symbol of Russia's rich heritage.

*Chesterfield Parish Church (the Twisted Spire), Derbyshire, England, fourteenth century.*

*The Cathedral of Vasily the Blessed, Moscow, Russia. Barma and Postnik Yakovlev, 1561.*

*Sketch your own ideas for a spire, minaret or civic tower. Does it have any cultural connection to where you live?*

Copenhagen Stock Exchange, Børsen, Denmark. Lorentz and Hans van Steenwinckel the Younger, 1640.

Shown here are a variety of typical **street profiles.** A street profile shows how the surrounding buildings interact and shape the character of the street. In my examples, you can see how the stepped facades, balconies, arcades, roof lines and basements all affect the streets' distinctive qualities.

*Draw your own street profile in the space provided.*

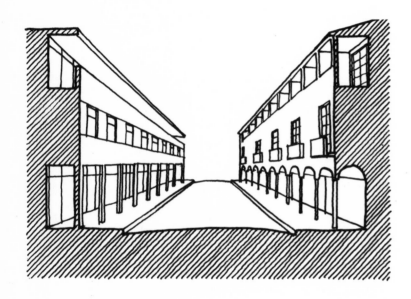

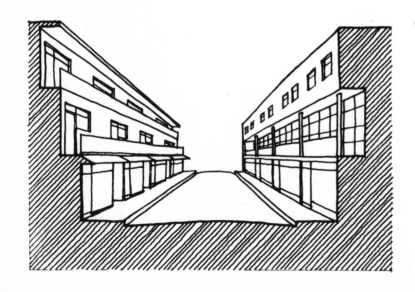

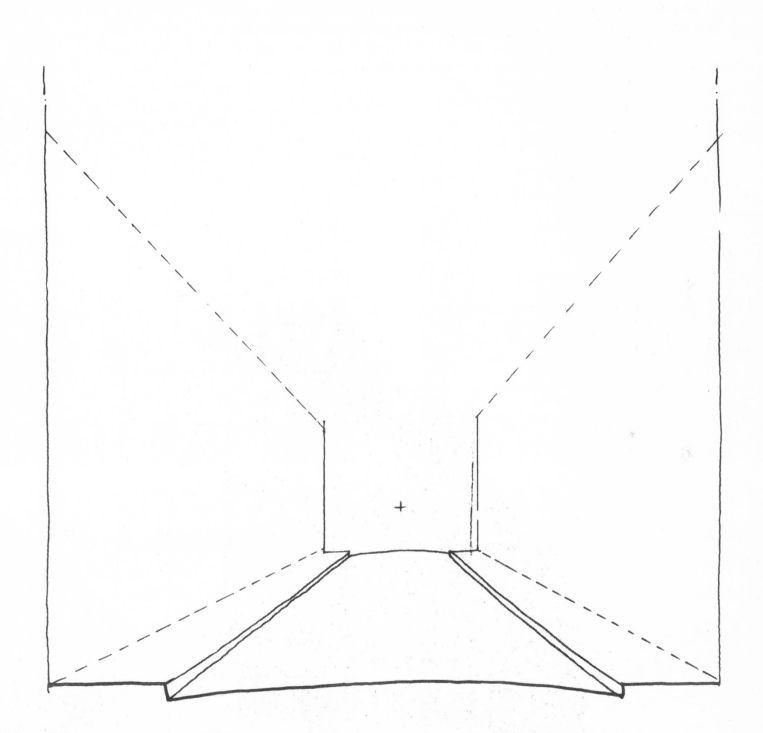

After World War II **new housing developments** were desperately needed in many European cities to replace the damage caused by the conflict. In post-war Britain, architects such as Peter and Alison Smithson and Ernö Goldfinger dedicated much of their practice to social housing and schools projects. Their buildings were uncompromising and were given the title of the 'New Brutalism', due to their raw appearance and use of unadorned concrete.

*Sketch your ideas for a social housing block within this outline of the Trellick Tower. Would you include green spaces? Sustainable technology?*

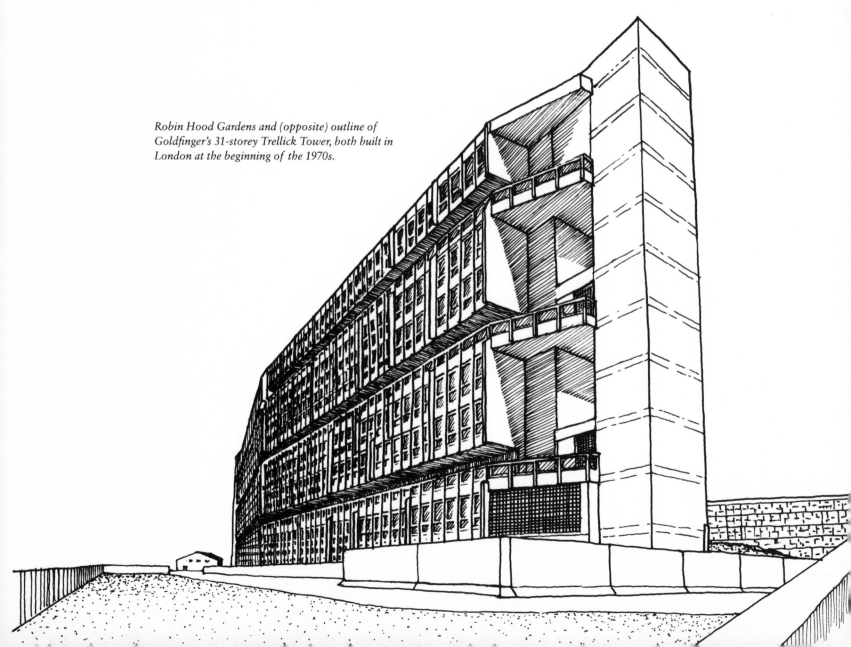

*Robin Hood Gardens and (opposite) outline of Goldfinger's 31-storey Trellick Tower, both built in London at the beginning of the 1970s.*

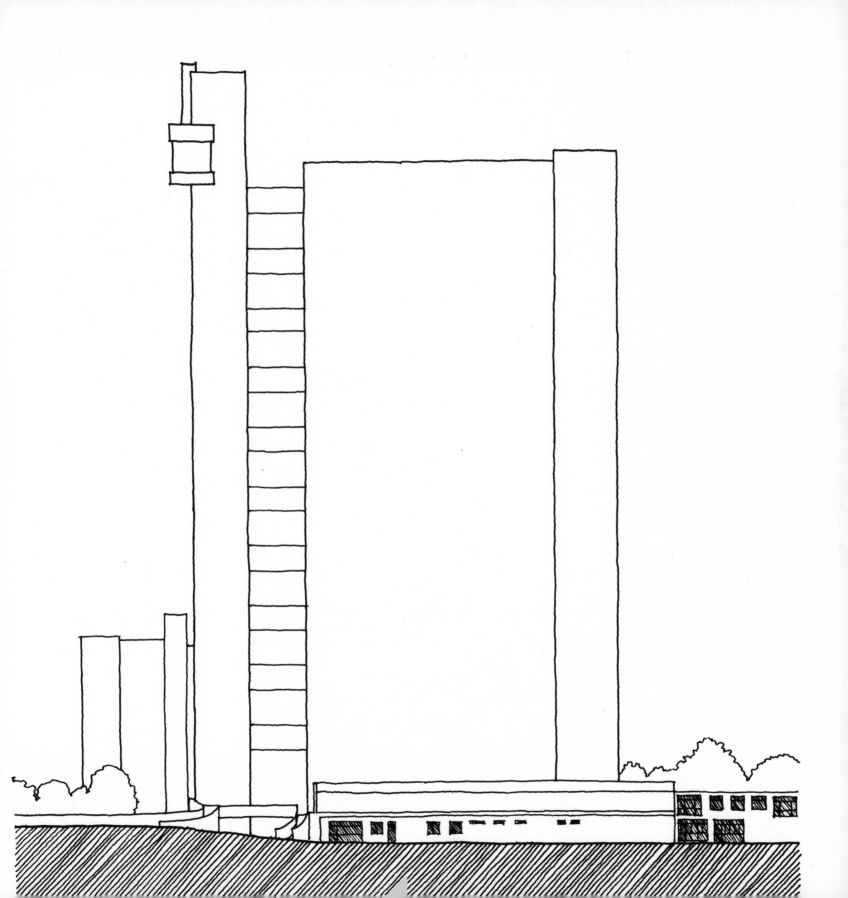

The designs of these modern **parliament buildings** utilized platonic forms (circles, squares, triangles) in the organization of their plans. In both buildings the circle is used as the 'democratic' meeting space for politicians to debate the future policies of their nations, with a variety of administration spaces surrounding the main hall.

*National Assembly Building, Dhaka, Bangladesh. Louis Kahn, 1982.*

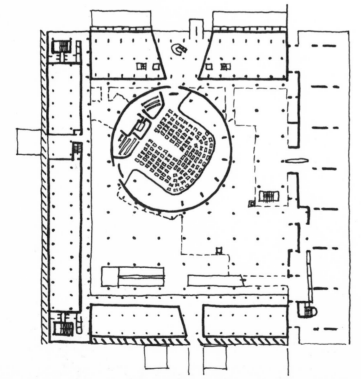

*Palace of Assembly, Chandigarh, India. Le Corbusier, 1955.*

*If you were to design a new parliament building using the shapes below, how would you organize the spaces in relation to one another? What would the main meeting areas be, and how would you promote democracy?*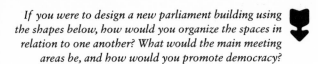

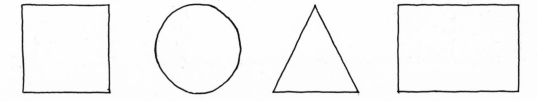

Famous for its sixteenth-century Renaissance and Baroque **merchant houses** is this square in Telc, Czech Republic. You will notice that all the dwellings share certain features – high gables, similar heights, arcades along the base and relatively symmetrical window patterns – while still being individual and unique.

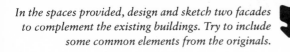

*In the spaces provided, design and sketch two facades to complement the existing buildings. Try to include some common elements from the originals.*

# 'Boulevard of the History of Architecture'

is a drawing by Hans Dieter Schaal from the 1970s, in which he constructed a no-scale plan image of a street, juxtaposing some of the world's most significant buildings in a linear route.

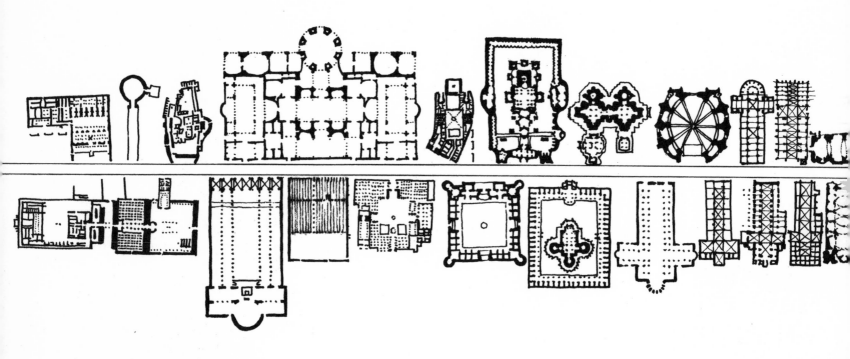

*I added some of my own favourite plans.*
*Why don't you do the same, then create your*
*own boulevard from scratch below?*

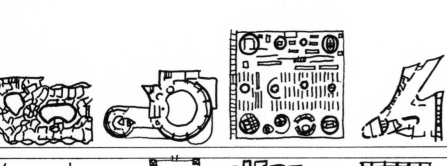

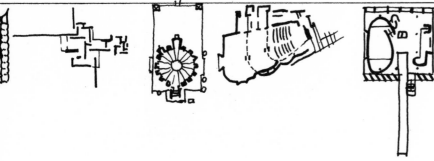

In their iconic 1972 book **'Learning from Las Vegas',** architects Denise Scott Brown, Robert Venturi and Steven Izenour analyzed the landscape of the Las Vegas strip. As it was a place and culture dominated by cars, they realized that signage was a very important factor for the casinos, motels and diners who were advertising themselves to their speeding customers. You will notice in the examples shown that the signage is composed of a much larger image or symbol that can be seen at long distance, and underneath there is more detailed information about the establishment and its services.

*Design your own motorway signage for a motel/diner. What facilities does it provide and what is on the menu?*

These two projects use **stacking blocks** on top of each other to create interesting spatial relationships. Designed for very different functions in different political environments, their construction is the one thing that they share in common.

*The Ministry of Highway Construction (now the Bank of Georgia), Tbilisi, Georgia. 19 Architect and Giorgi Chakhava for the Minister of Highway Construction, 1975.*

*Habitat 67 housing development, Montreal, Canada. Moshe Safdie, 1967.*

*Using similar block forms, sketch out some ideas*
*for a structure that relies on the stacking of simple*
*forms. What will its primary function be?*

The **roof terrace** of this unremarkable tower block in Beijing, China, became famous recently because the owner of the penthouse decided to convert his apartment's roof into a mountaintop retreat using rocks, rubble and shrubs. It took close to six years to complete but, as it did not have planning permission and was deemed to be unsafe, the owner was forced to remove it.

*If you had a penthouse on top of a tower and were allowed to build your fantasy roof terrace, what would you design?*

The **plan of Barcelona** expanded greatly in the nineteenth century, thanks mainly to the Spanish urban planner Ildefons Cerdà i Sunyer. Cerdà envisaged a grid of low-rise blocks with commercial spaces on the ground and first floors and living apartments above. In the centre of each block he planned gardens and green spaces. In practice, Cerdà's idealized use of urban space was hardly achieved, with nearly all the blocks being enclosed and few gardens surviving. Most of the courtyards today are occupied by car parks and workshops.

*Use the footprint of the blocks to draw how you would re-plan the courtyards.*

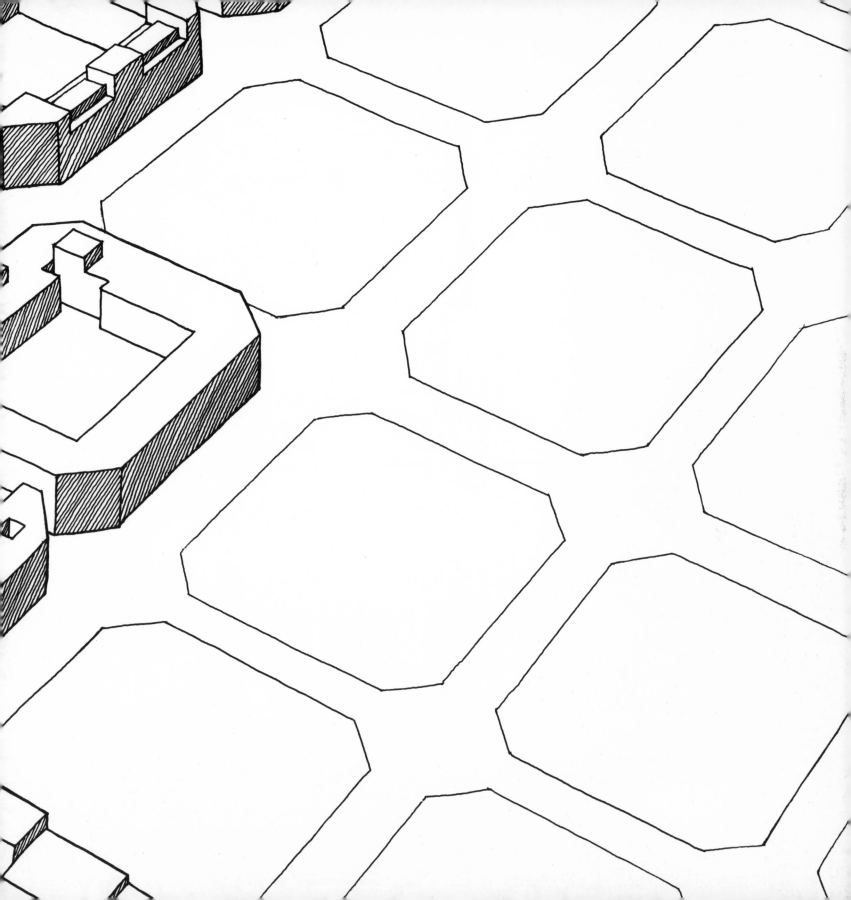

This **panorama collage** is composed of buildings from London and New York.

*Add your own iconic towers to the famous ones illustrated here.*

In their influential book **'Collage City',** published in 1978, Colin Rowe and
Fred Koetter rejected the grand utopian visions of the past in favour of cities that embraced
collision, superimposition, contamination and rich historical layering. Here I have used
fragments of London, Paris, New York and Barcelona to form a new collage city. If they became
one city, would it be called Ny-lon, Parcelona or maybe even New Barceldon? Would you include
parks, avenues, squares and monuments?

*Draw the new districts to join these
fragments and complete the city.*

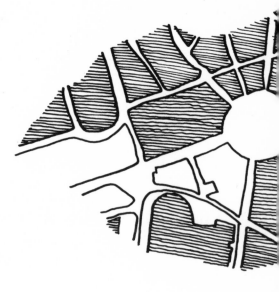

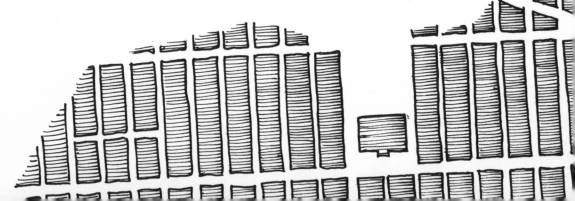

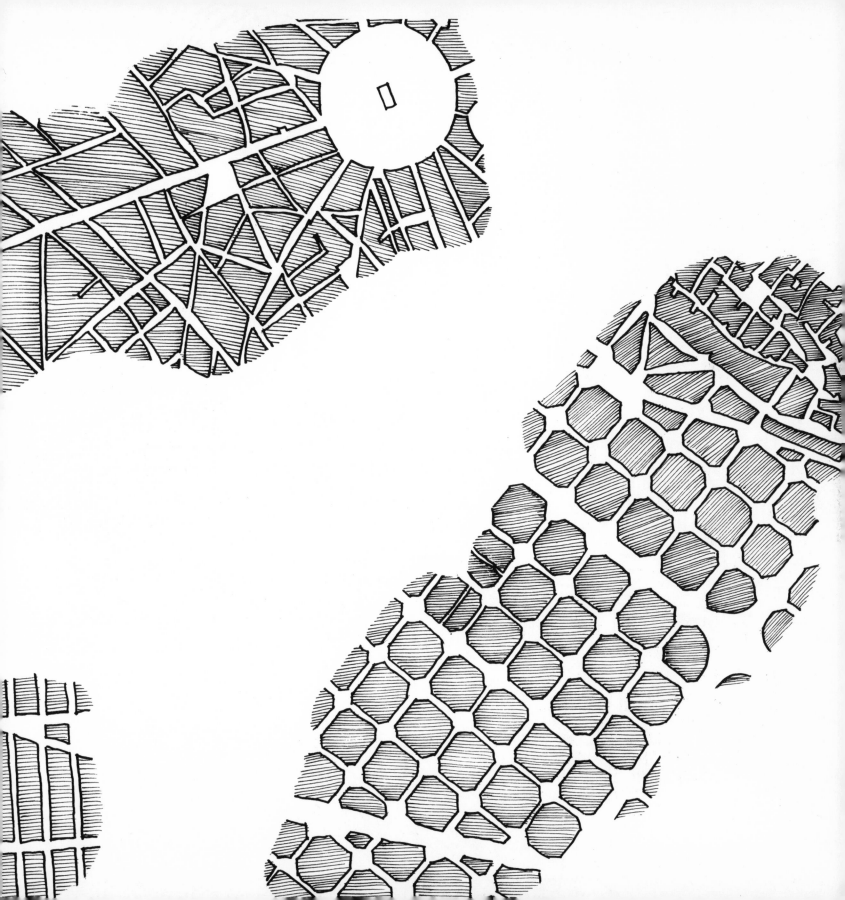

When the American architect **Louis Kahn** said 'The Street is a room by agreement', he was suggesting that streets were communal spaces that should serve the needs of the many. In recent times, proposals have been made for city centres to ban the use of private cars, thus opening up new possibilities for safer, cleaner and more active streets.

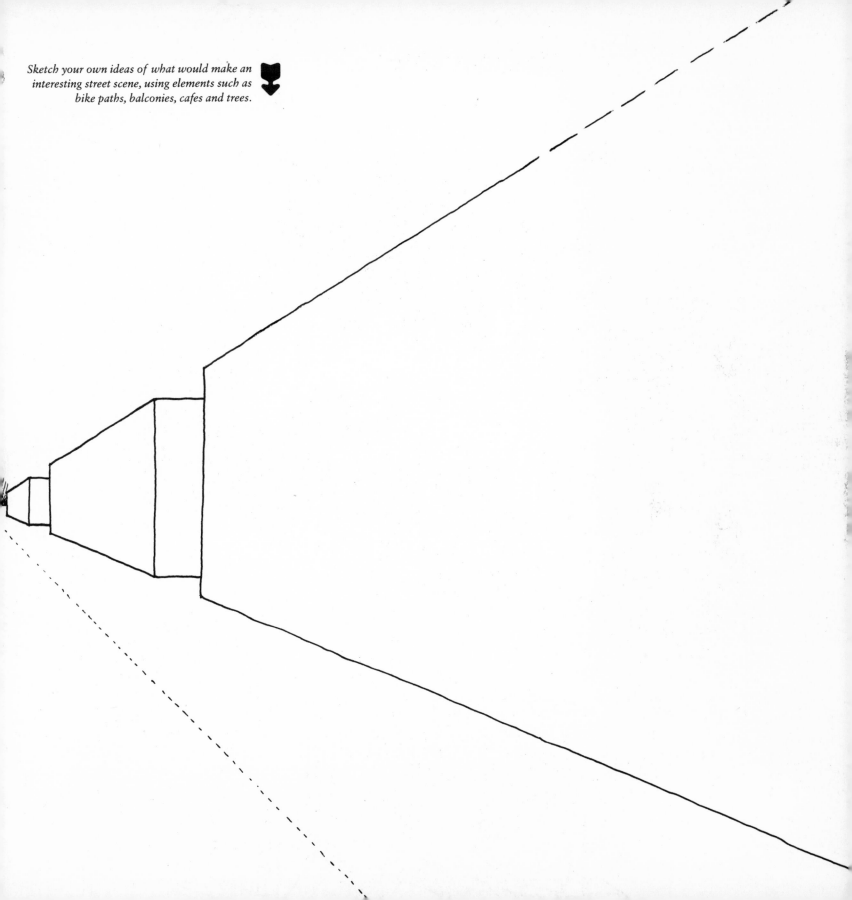

*Sketch your own ideas of what would make an interesting street scene, using elements such as bike paths, balconies, cafes and trees.*

Located within Manhattan's East Village is **Alphabet City,** so called because its avenues A, B, C and D are the only streets in New York to have single-letter names. In the fictional cityscape below I made a name from the buildings.

*Complete the city using the blocks to spell out your own name.*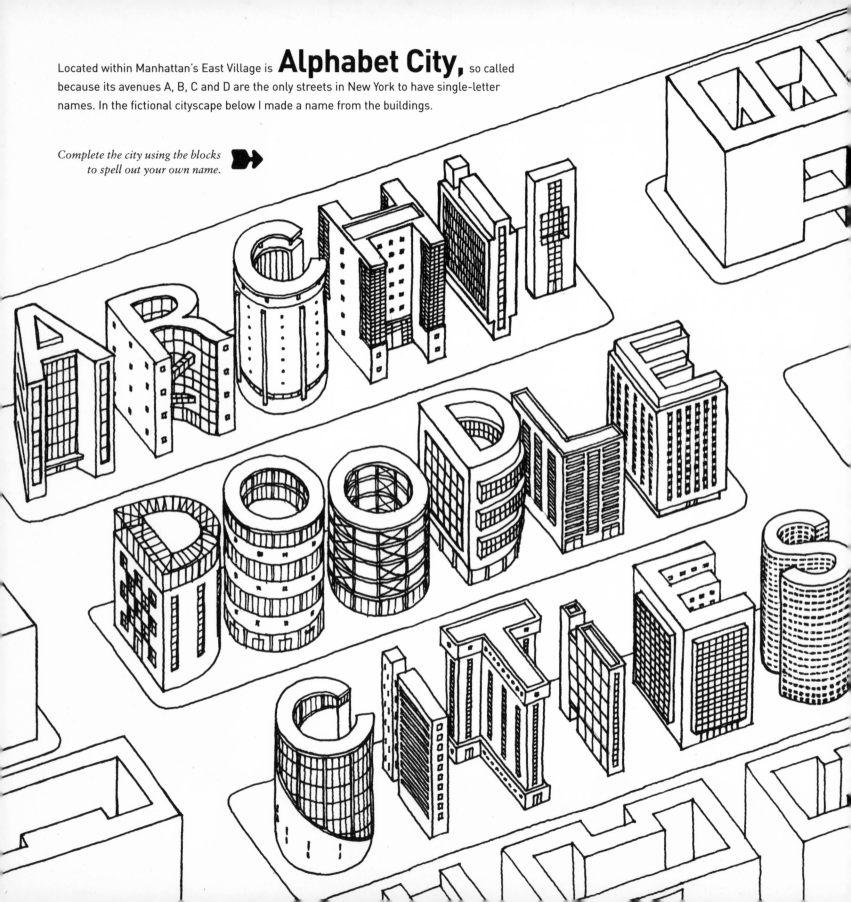

# Credits & acknowledgements

All of the drawings in the book have been created by the author especially for this publication; some are based on the original drawings of architects and artists, and these have been credited in the accompanying text where appropriate. In all cases, every effort has been made to credit the copyright holder, but should there be any omissions or errors the Publisher would be pleased to insert the appropriate acknowledgement in subsequent editions of this book.

Le Corbusier's Plan Voisin, Paris, and plan of the Palace of Assembly, Chandigarh © FLC/ADAGP, Paris and DACS, London 2016.

The author would like to give many thanks to Jane Tankard for all of her encouragement, inspiration and time spent giving feedback. Also thanks to Philip Cooper, Liz Faber and Gaynor Sermon at Laurence King Publishing for their help, support and editorial dedication, and to Matt Cox at Newman and Eastwood for designing the book.